Bedtime Bible Stories
for Catholic Children:
Loving Jesus through His Word

Mrs. Hermann Bosch

Study Aids by
Janet P. McKenzie

Biblio Resource Publications
108½ South Moore Street
Bessemer, MI 49911
2011

Previously published as *Bible Stories Told to "Toddles"* by Longmans, Green & Company, February 1910, Third Printing March 1916. *Nihil Obstat* – Remigius LaFort, S.T.L., Censor *Imprimataur* – John M. Farley, D.D., Archbishop of New York This edition: ©2011 by Janet P. McKenzie

ISBN 978-1-934185-39-1

Published by Biblio Resource Publications, Inc.
108½ South Moore Street, Bessemer, MI 49911
info@biblioresource.com

A Read Aloud Curriculum Enrichment Product
www.RACEforHeaven.com

Cover art ©zatletic – Fotolia.com

Printed in the United States of America

Introduction

These twenty Bible stories were originally published in serial form in a children's magazine, "The Messenger of the Sacred Heart." According to their author, "The tales are extremely simple and unadorned. They are real conversations of a real child and her mother . . ." Due to popular demand, the series was later (1910) published as a book, *Bible Stories Told to "Toddles,"*—being entitled after the author's pet name for her young daughter. A second series—finishing the Gospels—followed and was published in book form in 1911 as *When Toddles Was Seven.*

Continuing the spirit in which this series was originally published, it is strongly recommended that these stories be read aloud. After each reading, take time to discuss together the questions that follow the Bible story as well as the "Growing in Holiness" section. It is this section that contains the heart of the Bible story as here we learn how to live the message of the story in our daily lives—how we can grow in our love for our Lord and show our love for God in our daily life.

Then read the biblical passage in its entirety. To better familiarize ourselves with Holy Scripture—and to become more comfortable in the actual use of a Bible—help the child locate the passage in the Bible and read it directly from the book in question. (If your home does not have a Bible, now would be a good time to choose one together for purchase.)

If desired, review the pertinent sections of the catechism. The catechism questions are taken from the 1885 *Baltimore Catechism* while the brief lesson for adults is excerpted from the *Compendium* of the *Catechism of the Catholic Church* with references to the *Catechism of the Catholic Church* (CCC).

The name of the inquisitive little girl has been changed in this edition to "Carina," which means "dear little one." Additionally, some of the language of the original text has been updated. Note too that most of the Scripture citations within the text have been updated to the New American translation.

Remember as you read not to become a slave to the story. Allow for the gentle flow of the child's natural curiosity by pausing for questions when you see them arise. Part of the beauty of a read-aloud session is the spontaneous spiritual conversation that becomes a comfortable element of the time spent together.

May you enjoy discovering God's Word together. May your love for our beloved Savior increase with each story and may you grow together in holiness and intimacy with Jesus as you work to live out each lesson in your daily lives.

Janet P. McKenzie
May 13, 2011
Feast of Our Lady of Fatima

Contents

The Nativity

"Was it a happy birthday, Carina?"

"Oh, yes indeed, Mommy," the little girl replied, dropping her tired little head against her mother's shoulder, and sighing happily. "It was so nice, I can't remember it all. Sometimes, Mommy, when a whole lot of good things come at once, I just have to forget some of them till the next day."

"That's a very clever idea—you can make a joyful day last a long while if you think over only a part of it at a time."

"It's like keeping candies," laughed Carina, "and having some for a whole week 'stead of eating them all up the first chance. I had five boxes, Mommy, and sixteen other presents. Wasn't everybody good to me?"

"Yes, darling. As this *is* your birthday, do you know which story I think would be best tonight?"

Carina settled herself. "The story of Jesus' birthday—that's Christmas, Mommy."

"I'm not sure you'll keep awake long enough," said Mommy. "You've jumped about like a cricket all day."

"But, Mommy, I'm six years old. Of course I could keep awake for"—Carina thought a second—"well, for ever so long." She did not want to say any special length of time, because sometimes little children's eyelids will go down and stay down at the most unexpected times, no matter how much effort is made to keep wide awake and politely listening.

"Well, as my little girl said, Christmas Day is Jesus' birthday—the most wonderful, loving day in the whole year, the day God himself came into the world as a tiny infant."

"And Mary and Joseph went a long, long way," said Carina, "from where they lived in Nazareth, up to Bethlehem. It was very tiresome, but they had to pay a tax—what for, Mommy?"

"To the Roman government, Carina, that ruled the country of the Jews at that time. Taxes are paid to the government, that is, to those who rule cities or states, or whole countries, in order that the government may have money to pay for all its public works —like roads, and water-pipes, and in our days, schools and hospitals, besides.

"The Roman emperor, or Caesar Augustus as he was called, had sent out an order that everyone must give in his name and pay some money in whichever city he belonged. Now both Mary and Joseph belonged to the family of the Jewish King David, and Bethlehem was the City of David. That's why they left their little home in Nazareth and made the uncomfortable journey to Bethlehem in the winter time."

"And I remember," said Carina eagerly, "that St.

Joseph had a donkey for Mary to ride, so she wouldn't be too tired, Mommy. You told me that long ago. But St. Joseph walked, and it got awfully late because he could not go very fast over the hills. But Mommy, I'd rather you told it."

Her mother smiled.

"I'm delighted that my little girl knows the story so well. Yes, it grew late and cold, and many travelers passed Mary and Joseph and so reached Bethlehem ahead of them. When the Blessed Mother and St. Joseph arrived, the little city was crowded. Every possible resting place was already taken. There was not a single room left for the mother of Jesus."

"It must have been awful, Mommy. Once when we were traveling, every hotel was full, and we drove all around and it got dark, and I was hungry and oh, so sleepy! Don't you remember?"

"Yes, dear. There is a terribly lonely feeling about having nowhere to go. Mary and Joseph wandered about Bethlehem, looking for shelter and finding none. Neither complained, but St. Joseph's heart grew heavy as he realized that they might have to spend the cold night out in the open air. As he was about to give up the search for a resting-place, someone took pity on him and told him of a cave outside the city, where cattle slept and there were at least a roof and some protection from the chilly night winds. Tired as they were, Mary and Joseph gladly went on to this poor cave, grateful to the man who told them of it."

"And there were mangers in the cave," added Carina, "because Baby Jesus was wrapped in swaddling clothes and laid in a manger. And he was a real baby, like all little babies, only he was God besides."

"Exactly, darling. Let me see, how far were we?"

"They went to the cave. It was an awful place to send the Blessed Mother, I think, but she and St. Joseph weren't cross about it, were they, Mommy?"

"No, they were glad that some sort of shelter was possible for them. You see, Jesus chose to come into this world very, very poor, and so he willed to be born in the cave, which was a home only for cattle. No other people ever lived in it, but Mary and Joseph were resting there when Jesus was born.

"Well—Bethlehem lies in a hilly country, Carina, and out on the quiet hills many sheep were pastured. There were shepherds for the day and other shepherds for the night, who watched the flocks so that no harm might come to them."

"The big sheep and the little lambs," said Carina softly. "I think they were nice men, Mommy, because they could not have shepherds who would hurt little lambs."

"No, they were good simple men, living in sweet fresh air under the open sky. Their work was always to guard the flocks at night, so they knew how the sky looked at different seasons of the year. They knew how the stars shone and how the moon shone. They knew how dawn broke and how the sun rose to hide the stars by its own shining being so much stronger. They were not people easily frightened or upset."

"Not nervous people," said Carina, who had heard

excitable persons excused as being "nervous."

"No," smiled her mother, "not the least bit nervous. But in the middle of that night when Jesus was born, the shepherds were astonished to see a great light blazing in the sky, which was not the light of moon, or stars, or sun. It was more beautiful than any light the world had ever seen, and the men stood still, staring in greater and greater wonder."

"If we'd only been there, Mommy!" said Carina earnestly.

"Suddenly, as the light still grew, a beautiful angel stood beside the shepherds, and they became very much frightened indeed, for they knew not what to think. But the radiant angel spoke softly to them, saying, 'Do not be afraid,'[1] and immediately all their dread passed away. Then the angel went on to tell them that he brought them glad news: that Christ, the Savior, was born and lying in a manger, where they would find him wrapped in swaddling clothes."

"The Blessed Mother was very poor," said Carina sadly, "and there was no pretty nursery for Baby Jesus."

"But she would not have taken all the riches in the world, darling, for that little Child who was God."

"And even the ox and the ass that were in the cave knew he was God, didn't they, Mommy? Because they knelt down before the manger."

"Yes, darling. There is a story that the beasts knew the Creator of all was lying in their midst, and that they knelt in adoration and warmed the tiny Infant

---

[1] Luke 2:10

with their breath. It is a beautiful idea. Meanwhile, the shepherds out upon the hills were listening to the great song of a whole multitude of angels. Do you know what those angels sang, Carina? See if you can tell me?"

"'Glory to God in the highest and on earth peace to those on whom his favor rests,'"[2] answered the child.

"That was the song the shepherds heard until the angels departed again. It was a new song, dear, which put away anger and meanness and revenge—"

"That's getting even, Mommy, isn't it?"

"You might call it that. It's making others suffer at our hands because we suffered at theirs. It's a dreadful thing, Carina. People who try to take revenge are daring to do what only God should do. And people who hate others and wish to make them unhappy, can't receive that beautiful message brought by the angels. They sang of glory to God first, and then of peace to the whole world if it would have good will toward men. The Prince of Peace, our Savior, was born, and his coming was to end all anger and quarrels and unkindness for those who loved him. He came so humble, and little and helpless, Carina, to teach us how ugly pride and self-assurance are in the eyes of God. That tiny Child is to lead us to heaven, and those who follow a child must be gentle and tender. I'm sure the shepherds were peaceful and full of good will because to them the angels first brought their message."

"And the shepherds went and found Baby Jesus,

---

[2] Luke 2:14

like the angels said," remarked Carina with great satisfaction. "And some of the little lambs went with them, right to the crib where Baby Jesus was."

"Yes, dear. The simple shepherds went joyfully and in great haste to adore this Child for whom the world had been waiting for thousands of years. And they found him in the manger, with the Blessed Mother and St. Joseph kneeling by him. As soon as the shepherds saw him, they too fell upon their knees and adored him. How still it must have been, Carina!"

"Like you hold your breath," said Carina, "when you are too glad!"

"You see, darling, that little cave had become the palace of the King of heaven and earth, and the humble, holy Mary of Nazareth was the Mother of God. Herod and Caesar in their grand houses didn't know what had happened. But the poor shepherds knew, and so they knelt and prayed in great joy and wonder, and thankfulness because God the Father had shown his love for us by sending Jesus his Son as a Child into the world."

"It's a lovely story, Mommy."

"The story of Jesus' birthday, darling, the day he gave us himself, and asked our love in return."

"And the three kings? Tell me about them, Mommy."

"They didn't come until twelve days after Christmas, sweetheart. The next story shall be about them."

Discussion Questions

1. Why did Jesus wish to come into the world as a poor infant? Why did he will to be born in a cave? What lessons can this teach us?
2. Imagine what it might have felt like to be a shepherd the night Jesus was born. How might you have felt to see the bright star? The angel? Would you have believed the angel's message? Would you have gone to adore the Christ Child? If so, describe what you would have seen.
3. "Those who follow a child must be gentle and humble." Why is this statement true? Why do you think the shepherds left the manager with hearts full of peace and good will?

Growing In Holiness

Carina's mother describes "revenge" as "getting even" or "making others suffer at our hands because we suffered at theirs." Why is this a "dreadful thing"? Have you ever wanted to see someone else suffer because you had been hurt? What does Jesus ask us to do in this situation? What resolution can you make now to avoiding seeking revenge (or "getting even") next time? Make this a point to consider each night before going to bed: Did I hang onto my anger today or try to get even with anyone? Was I kind and forgiving as Jesus wishes me to be?

📖 Searching Scripture – Luke 2:1-20

In those days a decree went out from Caesar Augustus that the whole world should be enrolled. This was the first enrollment, when Quirinius was governor of Syria. So all went to be enrolled, each to his own town. And Joseph too went up from Galilee from the town of Nazareth to Judea, to the city of David that is called Bethlehem, because he was of the house and family of David, to be enrolled with Mary, his betrothed, who was with child. While they were there, the time came for her to have her child, and she gave birth to her firstborn son. She wrapped him in swaddling clothes and laid him in a manger, because there was no room for them in the inn.

Now there were shepherds in that region living in the fields and keeping the night watch over their flock. The angel of the Lord appeared to them and the glory of the Lord shone around them, and they were struck with great fear. The angel said to them, "Do not be afraid; for behold, I proclaim to you good news of great joy that will be for all the people. For today in the city of David a savior has been born for you who is Messiah and Lord. And this will be a sign for you: you will find an infant wrapped in swaddling clothes and lying in a manger." And suddenly there was a multitude of the heavenly host with the angel, praising God and saying:

"Glory to God in the highest and on earth
peace to those on whom his favor rests."

When the angels went away from them to heaven, the shepherds said to one another, "Let us go, then, to Bethlehem to see this thing that has taken place, which the Lord has made known to us." So they went in haste and found Mary and Joseph, and the infant lying in the manger. When they saw this, they made known the message that had been told them about this child. All who heard it were amazed by what had been told them by the shepherds. And Mary kept all these things, reflecting on them in her heart. Then the shepherds returned, glorifying and praising God for all they had heard and seen, just as it had been told to them.

✓ **Checking the Catechism**

1. *What are angels?* Angels are bodiless spirits created to adore and enjoy God in heaven.
2. *On what day was Christ born?* Christ was born on Christmas Day in a stable in Bethlehem, over two thousand years ago.

★REVIEW★ **Adult Catechism**

No. 60. The angels are purely spiritual creatures . . . They ceaselessly contemplate God face-to-face and they glorify him. They serve him and are his messengers. . . (See Nos. 328-333 and 350-351 in the CCC.)

The Three Kings

Carina's feelings were hurt; one of her little friends had presented her with a wonderful doll that would float in a basin of water, and had later on "taken it back." Carina's mother knew. Not because Carina told; Carina would not be mean. But her mother saw the doll and later missed it. Then when evening came, and Carina sat in Mommy's lap in the dusky bedroom, Carina's tears suddenly broke forth.

"What is the trouble, darling?"asked Mommy, in the voice that took half the trouble away at once.

"I—I can't tell. It would be tattling."

"Oh! Well, perhaps I can guess. Sometimes little girls make other little girls presents—not from their whole hearts, but in a sudden vain wish to please. Afterward, the fondness for the present grows to be much stronger than the vain desire to please, and at last the gift is wished back again."

"How do you know everything, Mommy?" asked Carina, in a whisper.

"I don't. Now listen, Carina. Yesterday you were happy, weren't you?"

"Yes, Mommy; of course," surprised at the question.

"And you had not received the doll that would float, had you?"

Carina's blue eyes studied Mommy's brown ones. In the twilight, Carina's grew very dark.

"No," seriously. "Why?"

"Because, if Carina could be happy yesterday without the doll, she must forget she ever had it, and be happy today. Won't that be best?" coaxingly.

Carina considered. After a moment, a light shone in her shadowy eyes.

"It would be, Mommy. But it's hard to forget." Carina hid her face against her mother, wishing she could at once do what Mommy suggested.

"Yes," agreed Mommy, "it is hard. But, sometimes, dear, it is very hard for the other person not to want things back. Whenever you give anything, Carina, be sure to give it entirely."

Carina sat up straight.

"Mommy," said she eagerly, "the three kings did not want their gifts back. And you promised, the other night, to tell me that story very soon."

"Very well, dear. Let me see—I'm afraid you can't remember the kings' names, can you?"

Carina sighed. "I know one—Gaspar the Greek. The others are so awful hard, Mommy."

"That's a very good beginning. Besides Gaspar the Greek, there were Balthazar the Egyptian, and Melchior the Hindu. They had all seen the star—each in his own country, far away from the others—and each started upon his journey in perfect faith that at the end of it he would find Jesus."

"And they weren't afraid," added Carina impressively. "Not of the ride on those high camels, nor the hot, shining sun on the sands, nor the dreadful dark nights."

"Why weren't they afraid, Carina?"

"Because they always saw the star, Mommy. You say it was brighter and brighter when the sky got darker and darker."

"Like faith, darling, which shines best when we are in trouble and sorrow. So they traveled on, very silently, no doubt, for they had much to think about. Remember, they were three kings, and had left a great deal of responsibility behind them at home. But they did not worry and fret over what might happen while they were away. They knew that God who had commanded them to follow the star would care for their countries and their people."

"That's what you call confidence, Mommy, isn't it?"

"Yes. Confidence in God. Everyone needs it, dear. Carina, and Mommy, and the three kings and all."

"I think so, too," sadly, remembering how very little "confidence" she had had when Amy Deans had walked home with the reclaimed doll.

"After a long, long journey they met—Gaspar, Balthazar, and Melchior. They recognized each other at once, although they had never met before. And they thanked God for the meeting and proceeded on the way together, full of joy that soon they would see the

Christ and offer to him their gifts."

"Gold, frankincense, and myrrh," said Carina, for the story was reaching the part where she felt more at home. "But they went to naughty Herod, Mommy, and almost did not find Jesus at all."

"No," smiling. "They went to Jerusalem to see Herod and to ask him where Christ should be born, because the star had disappeared, and they no longer knew the way."

"And Herod was jealous. He didn't want Jesus to be king, did he?"

"No, darling. The three kings' visit disturbed him very much indeed, especially when he had the great scholars get out their famous books and study all they could find about Jesus the Messiah. They told Herod Jesus would be born in Bethlehem. So he bade the kings go find the Child, and then return to Jerusalem. Herod pretended he wanted to visit Jesus and adore him, too."

"But he didn't, Mommy. Herod meant to kill the baby Jesus," sadly.

"Yes. But God the Father did not will that Jesus should die then. He warned the three kings in a dream not to have anything more to do with Herod after they had found Jesus. And as they had obeyed God in following the star, they obeyed him about not seeing Herod again. They did not argue or question."

Carina sighed. Obeying without a question was so very hard, sometimes. Mommy patted her, understanding the cause of the sigh.

"From Jerusalem they had not very far to go,"

Mommy continued. "After the difficulties of their journey and the bitter trial of having the star disappear for a while, and all their weariness and waiting, they were rewarded by finding Jesus at Bethlehem."

"With Mary, his mother. Like the shepherds."

"Like the shepherds. Nobody ever looks for him and fails to find him—kings and shepherds, rich and poor, little children like Carina, big people like Daddy and me—everybody. And finding him, the three kings knelt down and adored him, offering their gifts."

"I wish I had gold and frankincense and myrrh for Jesus," whispered Carina softly.

"You have your little heart to give him, and that is the best gift of all—your little heart, and all the hours of the day. Jesus prized the love, not the gold, and the adoration, not the frankincense."

"And the Blessed Mother put the things away for Baby Jesus. But he knew all about them, Mommy, didn't he?"

"Yes, darling; he knew everything, because he was always God. And after adoring him, the kings went back to their own countries, to tell that he had come. They did not belong to the Jews, as the shepherds did. Do you remember what the Jews called people who did not have their faith?"

"No, Mommy," a little bit embarrassed.

"They called them Gentiles. The three kings belonged to the Gentiles. And when they found Jesus, they were the first of those strangers to see the Messiah. So imagine with what joy, Carina, they returned to their homes!"

"But Jesus was glad to see them, too, Mommy. And I believe Jesus' mother was glad, and smiled, don't you?"

"Surely, Carina. And the Blessed Mother always smiles upon those who love her Son, because she loves him best of all herself."

And then, with a very tender smile of her own, her mother laid the drowsy Carina in her bed.

Discussion Questions

1. Did you ever give someone something and later regret it and want it back? Has anyone ever given something to you and later taken it back? Why is it important to learn to "give entirely"?

2. Do you too have trouble "obeying without question"? Why it is hard to obey cheerfully, immediately, and completely? Why is it important to learn to do so?

3. Carina's mother states, "Nobody ever looks for him [Jesus] and fails to find him." Where and how can we look for Jesus? What do we gain in our search? What do we gain when we find him? What do we lose if we refuse to look for and find Jesus? Meditate today for several minutes on the Fifth Mystery of the Joyful Mysteries of the rosary.

Growing In Holiness

You too can (and should!) give your heart to Jesus. Each day offer him your trials, sufferings, and joys.

Try to make small sacrifices for him each day. You
may wish to memorize and pray the following offering prayer each morning.

My God, I offer up to You
My soul and heart—and my mind too;
And all I do or hear or say
And all my work and all my play.
Amen.

Searching Scripture – Matthew 2:1-12

When Jesus was born in Bethlehem of Judea, in the
days of King Herod, behold, magi from the east arrived
in Jerusalem, saying, "Where is the newborn King of
the Jews? We saw his star at its rising and have come
to do him homage." When King Herod heard this, he
was greatly troubled, and all Jerusalem with him.
Assembling all the chief priests and the scribes of
the people, he inquired of them where the Messiah
was to be born. They said to him, "In Bethlehem of
Judea, for thus it has been written through the
prophet:

'And you, Bethlehem, land of Judah, are by no
means least among the rulers of Judah; since
from you shall come a ruler, who is to shepherd
my people Israel.'"

Then Herod called the magi secretly and ascertained
from them the time of the star's appearance. He sent
them to Bethlehem and said, "Go and search diligent-
ly for the child. When you have found him, bring me
word, that I too may go and do him homage." After

their audience with the king they set out. And behold, the star that they had seen at its rising preceded them, until it came and stopped over the place where the child was. They were overjoyed at seeing the star, and on entering the house they saw the child with Mary his mother. They prostrated themselves and did him homage. Then they opened their treasures and offered him gifts of gold, frankincense, and myrrh. And having been warned in a dream not to return to Herod, they departed for their country by another way.

✓ Checking the Catechism

1. *What are we commanded to do by the fourth Commandment?* We are commanded by the fourth Commandment to honor, love, and obey our parents in all that is not sin.

2. *Are we bound to honor and obey others than our parents?* We are also bound to honor and obey our bishops, pastors, magistrates, teachers, and other lawful superiors.

3. *What is forbidden by the fourth Commandment?* The fourth Commandment forbids all disobedience, contempt, and stubbonness towards our parents or lawful superiors.

✱REVIEW✱ Adult Catechism

Nos. 460-461. Parents . . . have the first responsibility for the education of their children . . . Parents do this mainly by example, prayer, family catechesis and participation in the life of the Church. (See CCC Nos. 2221-2231 and 2252-2253.)

The Presentation

"When Jesus was forty days old . . ." began Mommy.

"Forty days," Carina thoughtfully repeated. "That was still a very little baby, Mommy."

"Yes, dear, a very little baby in the Blessed Mother's arms. Well, there was a Jewish law that every first-born child, if it were a boy, belonged especially to God; and that fathers and mothers must carry such children to the temple and make an offering there in place of actually giving the child himself to the temple."

"I don't understand, Mommy," said Carina, who enjoyed the delicious privilege of asking her mother as many questions as she pleased.

"I'll try to explain," said Mommy, stroking the perplexed wrinkles out of Carina's forehead. "God had permitted an offering to be made which he had declared would redeem—buy back, as it were—the first-born from his obligation to dedicate himself entirely to the service of God in the temple. Rich people gave gold. Poor people like the Blessed Mother and St. Joseph offered two turtle doves or a pair of pigeons."

"What did Mary and Joseph offer for Baby Jesus?" asked Carina eagerly.

"What do you think, dear?"

"They might have given some of the gold the kings brought." Carina was thinking with all her might. "But no. The Blessed Mother could not give what had been given to Baby Jesus; that wouldn't be fair, Mommy."

Mommy smiled.

"They were so awful poor," Carina continued, "they must have given the doves." And Carina sighed. How much she wished the Holy Family had had everything that was rich and beautiful in this world!

"Don't sigh, little one. The doves were, in their gentleness and dependence, much more fitting the meek mother of Jesus. And all the things lacking to Mary and Joseph were the earthly things upon which they placed no value whatever. They had God; with him they could feel neither want nor deprivation."

"Like I feel with you, Mommy," murmured Carina, her heart shining in her eyes.

"Only much more, darling. Perhaps, dear, that trust little children feel in their mothers is the very nearest to the perfect faith the saints have in God. Anyway it seems the best comparison we can make, with our poor little hearts and minds. Perhaps it's why Jesus once said we must all become as little children if we expected to get to heaven."[3]

"But like good children," Carina hastened to explain. In her opinion, mothers were much nearer

---

[3] See Matthew 18:3.

heaven than children. Weren't children naughty, and sometimes had to be punished?

"Yes, good children. Obedient, trusting children. The Blessed Mother was the most obedient of all God's children. It was an act of simple, humble obedience when she took Baby Jesus to the temple and presented him as though he were subject to the Lord like other children. He was God, and therefore had made the law which he and his mother kept. Can't you imagine them going along the street, Carina, in the morning sunshine—Jesus, Mary and Joseph?"

Carina closed her eyes.

"Yes, I can, because I've seen the picture down in your room, and when I shut my eyes, Mommy, I can imagine it. The Blessed Mother's eyes so soft, and Baby Jesus asleep, and two white doves. Did they coo, like the doves I heard in the country?"

"Perhaps. And St. Joseph was the protecting figure over all. You can see how thoughtful and tender he was, if you look into his face. So they reach the temple. They pass within the doors without the idle persons standing about suspecting who they are. The people entirely taken up with earthly business can't recognize Jesus, no matter how closely they approach him. But within the temple it was different. There were two souls waiting for the Child Jesus there. They knew whom the Blessed Mother held in her arms."

"Who were the two, Mommy?" asked Carina, eagerly.

"One was Simeon, a man who was waiting upon earth simply until the day when God should show him the Christ, his Son."

"That was Baby Jesus," Carina declared, pleased that she was understanding all her mother said.

"Yes. Simeon took Jesus from the Blessed Mother and blessed God that he had permitted his faithful servant to see that day. He prayed that God would now let him depart in peace, because having seen Jesus, he had seen the salvation of all God's people. Then Simeon blessed Mary and Joseph and told the mother that a sword would pierce her heart."

"What did he mean, Mommy?"

"His words were a prophecy of the sorrow and sufferings that would come to Mary through the Passion of Jesus. Every mother suffers each grief her child must bear, but Mary, the mother of Jesus, as God created her the most perfect of human beings, loved and suffered more deeply than any other creature could."

"Was Mary frightened? "Carina asked.

"No. She wasn't afraid of the will of God. Simeon's words no doubt revealed to her that her life was to be the life of the Mother of Sorrows, but she knew God's grace would never fail her."

"Confidence," whispered Carina, who had very thoroughly mastered this "big word."

"Yes. And confidence brings courage, and courage —what?" curious to discover whether Carina would remember.

Carina laughed mischievously.

"You thought I'd forgotten, Mommy, but I remember—courage brings perseverance," and there was only a very slight lisp.

"Excellent! Now we mustn't take too long with our story. Besides Simeon, there was Anna waiting in the temple. She was very old—eighty-four—and had spent most of that long life fasting and praying in the temple. Anna recognized Jesus, too, and rejoiced and praised God. Then the little ceremony was over. The Holy Family left. Soon they were out of Jerusalem, on the way towards their home."

Carina was quite tired. "On the way home," she murmured contentedly. "I don't remember the name of the place just now, Mommy?"

"Nazareth," whispered Mommy, as the drooping eyelids closed.

Did Carina hear? Anyway, she smiled in her sleep.

Discussion Questions

1. Discuss the following quotation from page 20: "Perhaps, dear, that trust little children feel in their mothers is the very nearest to the perfect faith the saints have in God." Do you trust your parents to take care of you? Do you trust God to take care of you? What can we do to increase our trust in God—pray more often, worry less, fast, receive the Sacraments of Penance and Reconciliation and Holy Eucharist more often?

2. Have you suffered and undergone trials in your life? Do you know of anyone who has suffered

greatly either through illness, injury, poverty, or persecution? What is the purpose of Christian suffering?

3. Confidence in God brings courage which, in turn, yields perseverance. How might our confidence in God give us courage and help us to practice the virtue of fortitude?

✝ Growing In Holiness

"The people entirely taken up with earthly business can't recognize Jesus, no matter how closely they approach him" (page 21). Watch for evidence of the love of Jesus in the world—in nature, and in the faces, concern, and needs of other people. Remember that Jesus promised us that ". . . whatever you did for one of these least brothers of mine, you did for me" (Matthew 25:40b). Recognize Jesus in others; share with him and help him as much and as often as you can! (Even a smile means a lot!)

📖 Searching Scripture – Luke 2:22-38

When the days were completed for their purification according to the law of Moses, they took him up to Jerusalem to present him to the Lord, just as it is written in the law of the Lord, "Every male that opens the womb shall be consecrated to the Lord," and to offer the sacrifice of "a pair of turtledoves or two young pigeons," in accordance with the dictate in the law of the Lord.

Now there was a man in Jerusalem whose name was Simeon. This man was righteous and devout, awaiting the consolation of Israel, and the holy Spirit was upon him. It had been revealed to him by the holy Spirit that he should not see death before he had seen the Messiah of the Lord. He came in the Spirit into the temple; and when the parents brought in the child Jesus to perform the custom of the law in regard to him, he took him into his arms and blessed God, saying:

"Now, Master, you may let your servant go
    in peace, according to your word,
for my eyes have seen your salvation,
    which you prepared in sight of all the peoples,
a light for revelation to the Gentiles,
    and glory for your people Israel."

The child's father and mother were amazed at what was said about him; and Simeon blessed them and said to Mary his mother, "Behold, this child is destined for the fall and rise of many in Israel, and to be a sign that will be contradicted (and you yourself a sword will pierce) so that the thoughts of many hearts may be revealed." There was also a prophetess, Anna, the daughter of Phanuel, of the tribe of Asher. She was advanced in years, having lived seven years with her husband after her marriage, and then as a widow until she was eighty-four. She never left the temple, but worshiped night and day with fasting and prayer. And coming forward at that very time, she gave thanks to God and spoke about the child to all who were awaiting the redemption of Jerusalem.

✓ **Checking the Catechism**

1. *What did Jesus Christ suffer (his Passion)?* Jesus Christ suffered a bloody sweat, a cruel scourging, was crowned with thorns, and was crucified.
2. *Why did Christ suffer and die?* Christ suffered and died for our sins.
3. *What lessons do we learn from the sufferings and death of Christ?* From the sufferings and death of Christ we learn the great evil of sin, the hatred God bears to it and the necessity of satisfying for it.

✦REVIEW✦ **Adult Catechism**

No. 392. Sin is "a word, an act, or a desire contrary to the eternal Law" (Saint Augustine). (See CCC Nos. 1849-1851 and 1871-1872.)

The Flight into Egypt

"Mommy, what does the 'slaughter of the Holy Innocents' mean?" asked Carina, bringing out the long phrase by a great effort.

"What do you think it means?" her mother returned, folding her arms about the little girl as she seated herself for a long, cozy talk by the bedside.

"I think Herod did it," Carina declared quite fiercely. She possessed a very vivid dislike for the cruel king.

"Yes; he commanded all the boy-babies two years old or less to be killed. You see, the three kings had visited Herod, talking about the Christ for whom they were seeking, and wicked Herod was terribly frightened. What could he think at the question, 'Where is the newborn King of the Jews?'"[4]

"Something greedy and mean," said Carina, with conviction.

"But what, exactly?"

Carina fidgeted. She did not remember exactly what. Mommy smiled softly.

---

[4] Matthew 2:2

"Don't you see that if someone had been born King of the Jews, Herod would be succeeded by that child?"

"And Herod didn't want to be put out," Carina explained.

"Most decidedly not. Herod lived only for the glory and comfort of this world. He did not understand that there was a higher kingdom than his: a kingdom of souls, a Kingdom of Heaven. He could not imagine that the Child for whom the wise men were looking would despise the wealth and the honors of this world. Herod thought only of earthly power. The Child would inherit his gold and luxury. Herod grew furious at these thoughts. Little as you are, you can understand that a person would have to be wild with anger and hatred in order to kill anybody."

"Yes," agreed Carina solemnly; "it is so very awful."

"Now imagine Herod working himself up to such an extent that he killed not one or two, but oh, so many! He was led on by the insane desire to destroy that Child so wonderful that a star showed the place of his birth; so mighty that kings came from afar to do him homage while he was a tiny, helpless Infant. Herod himself was a king. Nothing wonderful had happened at the time of his birth. Very few people knew of his existence until long years afterward. Herod realized these things. Surely the Child born in Bethlehem was dangerous to Herod's own glory and peace. He could not be an ordinary Child. But Herod, reckoning without God, determined to make sure of his throne and his kingdom at any price. He would kill the Child."

"But why did he kill so many, Mommy?"

"Because he did not know exactly where Mary and Joseph had taken Jesus, and Herod did not want to take any chances of the particular Child he wished to destroy escaping. You see, the wicked king followed only human reasons. He overlooked the fact that he could accomplish nothing which would interfere with the designs of God. So the cruel edict went forth—"

"What is an edict, please?"asked Carina, interrupting.

"A command that is a law. Herod's command, then, went forth, and all the little boys of the age he had ordered, in Bethlehem and all the nearby places, were slain."

"But Jesus was not," said Carina reassuringly.

"No. The Holy Innocents, as we call these young martyrs, were slain for him, and so many mothers were left weeping and desolate"—Carina nestled yet more closely in her mother's arms—"but Herod's wish had not been accomplished. Jesus was to live and teach and suffer for thirty-three years. God sent the warning to St. Joseph."

"An angel appeared to him," said Carina, always delighted when she could assist in the telling of the story.

"An angel appeared to him while he was asleep. And the angel said, 'Rise, take the child and his mother, flee to Egypt, and stay there until I tell you. Herod is going to search for the child to destroy him.'[5] Now, Carina, here we again have one of those star-

---

[5] Matthew 2:13

29

tling lessons of obedience. St. Joseph did not even wait until morning. The Bible expressly tells us that he arose directly, in the night, and, taking Jesus and Mary, began the journey into Egypt."

"St. Joseph was brave, Mommy," commented Carina.

"Brave and humble and, above all, obedient. You can see all through how the Holy Family was distinguished by their obedience. Mary and Joseph were always ready to sacrifice everything for God, and Jesus, the Son of God, became obedient, as the Bible says, 'to death, even death on a cross.'[6] He placed no limit to his obedience to the will of his Father."

"Because he loved his Father," Carina said happily. "When I think how I love you, Mommy, it's easy to do as I'm told."

Mommy dropped a kiss upon the upturned forehead.

"Yes, that is exactly the reason, darling. Let me see—where were we? Oh, yes; St. Joseph arose from his sleep, and taking the Child and the Blessed Mother, led them away to Egypt, beyond the power of Herod. In Egypt they dwelt as exiles, suffering many privations amongst strangers; away from their relatives, from their friends, surrounded by new customs, an unknown language, a false religion. Surely Mary and Joseph must have missed their temple, must have pined for the family devotions, the reverent, united celebrations of the Jewish feasts. But they never complained—" Mommy paused; a very deep

---

[6] Philippians 2:8

look in the little girl's eyes had caught her attention.

"They had Baby Jesus," said Carina softly, "so nothing else mattered, did it, Mommy?"

"No. They had him for whom the temple was built, him in whose honor the feasts were commanded. They had God, and so they did not feel the hardships they bore. They must have been very happy, Carina, even in Egypt. Wherever Jesus is must always be a bit of heaven; don't you think so?"

"Of course," earnestly. "Is it always dark in Egypt, Mommy?" curiously.

Mommy laughed. Carina had often heard grownup people use the expression "dark as Egypt."

"No indeed, darling; Egypt is often exceptionally bright and sunny. Only sometimes the night is intensely dark there; and besides, they have no twilight. Darkness follows daylight very suddenly, as it does this side of the world, too, when one goes to the south."

"I was afraid," said Carina, much relieved, "that Mary and Joseph and Baby Jesus would always have to be in the dark."

"No," Mommy returned thoughtfully. "And, do you know, I believe they wouldn't have minded darkness itself. You see Christ was one of the Holy Family, and so Mary and Joseph had with them the light that came into the world—the light 'which enlightens everyone.'[7]"

Carina did not quite understand this. Her mother caught the perplexed expression.

"Don't you remember, Carina? You know in the

---

[7] John 1:9

first chapter of St. John's Gospel we read about the 'true light.'[8] Whom does St. John mean?"

Carina smiled.

"Jesus, Mommy. I see what you mean. But the Blessed Mother did not keep Baby Jesus in Egypt for always, did she?"

"No. As soon as Herod died, God sent an angel to St. Joseph in his sleep, telling him he should return to the land of Israel; not to Judea, because the new king, Archelaus, might also fear the power of the Child Jesus, as Herod, his father, had done."

"Where did they go?" asked Carina faintly.

"To Nazareth, in Galilee. That is why Jesus was called 'the Nazarene.'"

Carina was very still. The story was finished just as the little girl slipped into the land of dreams.

Discussion Questions

1. Recall a time when you were angry—really angry. Looking back now, what might you have done differently to avoid doing angry things or saying angry words? Think of a code word you can use (or make a pact with a friend or family member to use this word for each other) to remind yourself (or each other) to ask Jesus or your guardian angel to help you control your anger.

2. Carina's mother says that Herod was "reckoning without God." How would your life change if you

---

[8] John 1:9

considered God and his wishes before ever acting or speaking?

3. "The Holy Family was distinguished by their obedience" (page 30). Here we see that it is important for us to learn obedience when we're young, not only because it is a necessary virtue for children but also that it is important for adults. In what ways must adults also be obedient? To whom must grown-ups be obedient?

✝ Growing In Holiness

"Wherever Jesus is must always be a bit of heaven" (page 31). In what areas of your life have you excluded Jesus? Do you talk with him often during the day? Do you praise and thank him often during the day? Are there some things (thoughts, words, habits) that you are trying to "hide" from Jesus? Try to see his action, his face, in all things and all people. Then we will truly experience heaven on earth!

📖 Searching Scripture – Matthew 2:13-23

When they [the Wise Men] had departed, behold, the angel of the Lord appeared to Joseph in a dream and said, "Rise, take the child and his mother, flee to Egypt, and stay there until I tell you. Herod is going to search for the child to destroy him." Joseph rose and took the child and his mother by night and departed for Egypt. He stayed there until the death of Herod, that what the Lord had said through the prophet might be fulfilled, "Out of Egypt I called my son."

When Herod realized that he had been deceived by the magi, he became furious. He ordered the massacre of all the boys in Bethlehem and its vicinity two years old and under, in accordance with the time he had ascertained from the magi. Then was fulfilled what had been said through Jeremiah the prophet:

"A voice was heard in Ramah,
    sobbing and loud lamentation;
Rachel weeping for her children,
    and she would not be consoled,
    since they were no more."

When Herod had died, behold, the angel of the Lord appeared in a dream to Joseph in Egypt and said, "Rise, take the child and his mother and go to the land of Israel, for those who sought the child's life are dead." He rose, took the child and his mother, and went to the land of Israel. But when he heard that Archelaus was ruling over Judea in place of his father Herod, he was afraid to go back there. And because he had been warned in a dream, he departed for the region of Galilee. He went and dwelt in a town called Nazareth, so that what had been spoken through the prophets might be fulfilled, "He shall be called a Nazorean."

✓ Checking the Catechism

1. *What is the fifth Commandment?* The fifth Commandment is: Thou shalt not kill.
2. *What are we commanded by the fifth Commandment?* We are commanded by the fifth Commandment to live in peace and union with our neighbor,

to respect his rights, to seek his spiritual and bodily welfare, and to take proper care of our own life and health.

3. *What is forbidden by the fifth Commandment?* The fifth Commandment forbids all willful murder, fighting, anger, hatred, revenge, and bad example.

✴REVIEW✴ Adult Catechism

No. 470. The fifth commandment forbids . . . direct and intentional murder and cooperation in it; direct abortion . . . direct euthanasia . . . suicide and voluntary cooperation in it. . . (See CCC Nos. 2268-2283 and 2321-2326.)

The Finding in the Temple

"Mommy," said Carina, with a shake of her curly head, "I think it was too awful that Jesus was lost, and how could the Blessed Mother live three whole days without him? If you had lost me, Mommy—" Carina closed her eyes, appalled at the picture of such woe.

In spite of herself, her mother tightened her arms about the chubby little creature upon her lap.

"It was different, Carina," said Mommy slowly; "we mustn't ever forget that point, when we study Jesus and his mother. They are our models, truly. We must try in big and little things to be as like them as we can, and then we must always still cling fast to the remembrance that Jesus was God—"

"Second Person of the Blessed Trinity, Son of the Father," supplemented Carina softly, in the way she often had of gently interrupting her mother to develop some thought— "Yes, Mommy?" expectant eyes raised to her mother's face.

"And Mary was of all creatures the nearest to God. She understood God better than any archangel could, she was holier than any of the host of heaven, and being better than anyone else and loving God more, she was called upon to suffer more than anyone else and differently from anyone else in the whole world and during all times."

"Except Jesus," Carina corrected.

"Jesus was not a creature, darling. He was God and Man, but always the Creator. And this Creator, having come into the world to fulfill the Law, did not avoid following its commands and practices. You see, all the Jewish boys went up to the temple when they were twelve years old. Families from towns and villages made the journey together, the women in one company, the men in another. Perhaps the Holy Family left Nazareth alone—just those three, Jesus, Mary and Joseph—but were soon joined by others going like themselves to Jerusalem. I like to think they started alone, don't you?—that they set out for the temple of the Father with only the angels as companions, distant for the time from people who might be rude, or not reverent, or perhaps, worst of all, carrying hidden sin—which to Jesus could not be hidden —upon their souls."

"Was it early in the morning, Mommy?"

"Probably. In the East—and the country in which Jesus lived was in the East—people are apt to do much in the very early morning. The air is cool and fresh then, and the sun, which later in the day can become disagreeably hot, is very welcome. So they began their journey about sunrise, I imagine, and it seems to me they were silent while they were alone, because the occasion was a serious one."

"Why, Mommy?" wonderingly. "I like to go places with you and Daddy."

"Yes, sweetheart. But here is one of the points where things are different again. Presenting Jesus in the temple at the age of twelve, meant to the Blessed Mother and St. Joseph that the Holy Childhood was at an end. They knew that Jesus was the Son of God. Hadn't the angels sung at his birth, and the shepherds and kings come to adore, besides the assurance of the angel to Mary, that her child would be the Son of the Most High? Knowing so much, and not knowing so much more, the day was a solemn one to Mary and Joseph when they formally acknowledged that the Divine Infancy was over. Why, Carina, do you know it will make my heart ache dreadfully, when I realize you are growing up?"

"I am," assented Carina proudly; "I'm growing every day."

Her mother sighed just the littlest sort of a sigh.

"Well—Jesus was growing up to fulfill his mission: The salvation of men. Simeon had told the Blessed Mother that a sword of grief would pierce her heart. Perhaps it was part of her greatest suffering that she was not told when this sword would come."

"Yes," Carina wisely agreed; "it's ever so much worse, Mommy, when something horrid is coming, and you can't ever tell when. Like the time I was awfully naughty, and couldn't be punished till the company went," and she grew very grave at this recollection. "It wasn't a real sword that Simeon meant, was it, Mommy?" anxiously.

"No. He meant that the Blessed Mother's sorrow for her Son would be sharp as the wound of a sword."

"But why was Jesus sad, Mommy, when he was going to the temple?"

"He was going, for the first time, about his Father's business, at the price of suffering on the part of his dear mother. Jesus knew that he would remain behind in the temple when his mother and St. Joseph started for their home in Nazareth. He knew Mary would seek him sorrowing—almost broken-hearted. He understood how terribly lonely, even alarmed, she would be. And he was not to warn her beforehand, because where God is concerned, not even the dearest and best of mothers may interfere. Carina, wouldn't it be very hard for you to have to cause me grief?"

"Yes," murmured Carina, but she hid her face against Mommy's shoulder, dimly conscious of occasions when small naughtinesses had made her mother look oh, so serious!

"I don't mean by trifles, sweetheart," smiled her mother, fully understanding the cause of the wee daughter's embarrassment.

"I couldn't bear to hurt you hard," said Carina, reassured.

"Well, that is what I mean by the solemnness of that going up to the temple: Jesus was about to grieve his loving mother and St. Joseph. So they journeyed pensively, all three, along the country road. But soon they met others. And we know that the Holy Family would be gracious and kind to all, putting aside their desire for silence and thought-fulness for the sake of the comfort and happiness of other travelers who would wish to be entertained on the way. Whenever you are tempted to be what you call impolite, Carina, remember that Jesus and Mary and Joseph were the most courteous and considerate of God's children. I'm sure that they chatted kindly and brightly with the simple country people about ordinary daily affairs. And when night came, they rested gratefully in what shelter they could find, never hinting that the Child was a guest such as no other, and for whose bidding the angels waited."

"And after days they reached Jerusalem, Mommy, and Jesus went into the temple and surprised the doctors," said Carina, who never forgot this point. It did seem so strange that the little Jesus—Baby Jesus as Carina often called him—could astonish those great, tall men with the thoughtful faces and long beards, down in that picture hanging in the library. But Carina knew why, of course: Jesus was different from other children, as her mother said, because Jesus was God.

"Yes, he asked those doctors of the Law questions which perplexed them completely, and he answered them with a wisdom which puzzled them yet more. But meantime Mary and Joseph left Jerusalem for home, Mary going with a party of women, Joseph joining a company of men. Each believed Jesus to be with the other, and traveling peacefully because of this idea, the first day passed. In the evening Mary and Joseph met. Imagine the quick question, Carina, the frightened looks, as neither Mary nor Joseph could say where Jesus was. Remember how perfectly they loved him, what joy he was to them, and your little heart may feel how dreadful was the thought that he was lost."

"Terrible," said Carina, so near tears that her mother hastened to console her.

"But they found him, darling, you know."

"Only after three days," said Carina sadly, "and I think three days is an awfully long time."

"Indeed they must have seemed dreadfully long to the Blessed Mother and St. Joseph. When they fled into Egypt, Jesus was with them, but as they hurried back to Jerusalem seeking the Child, their loneliness was extreme. They asked and they searched, but they did not find him on the way. Each hour that passed increased their dread that he was indeed lost and they might never see him again. By the time they reached Jerusalem and the temple, their hope was nearly gone—here was the last place where he might possibly be. Do you wonder, Carina, that the Blessed Mother said she sought him sorrowing?"

"No," Carina answered; "I'm sure she was so sorry, Mommy, that even St. Joseph couldn't comfort her."

"The hardest moment of all must have been just as they entered the temple, because if Jesus was not there, they knew of no other place where they might seek him. And in proportion to their previous worry and dread, Carina, was the joy at finding him. How their tired eyes must have lighted, when they saw

Jesus standing among the doctors, speaking the wisdom of God our Father! No doubt Mary and Joseph watched and listened for several minutes before they approached him, their prayers going out from rejoicing hearts in gratitude that they had found their beloved Child."

"When you want to speak just too much for anything, Mommy," said Carina understandingly, "you can't speak at all."

"That is true, dear. It took some time before Mary could ask Jesus tranquilly: 'Son, why have you done this to us? Your father and I have been looking for you with great anxiety.'[9] That was the cry of the mother who had been desolate for three days. And Jesus answered her, in the simple reason of his whole life, Carina: 'Did you not know that I must be in my Father's house?'[10] He meant his eternal Father, God. And Mary, the meek and the obedient, was satisfied and did not ask for explanations.

"Then they left the temple together, darling, Jesus, Mary and Joseph; Jesus had shown that the will of his heavenly Father came first and now he returned to Nazareth to be subject to his mother and St. Joseph. The Blessed Mother had received another lesson in the designs of God, had gone a little farther into the mission of her divine Son. Settling down quietly in the little house at Nazareth, she watched him grow in age and grace, while she kept all the words concerning him always in her heart."

---

[9] Luke 2:48
[10] Luke 2:49

"I'm going to try to keep all your words in my heart, Mommy, that are about Jesus and his mother," said Carina, "so I'll know them when I'm big."

"God bless my little girl," said Mommy. And then, she kissed Carina goodnight.

Discussion Questions

1. Have you ever been lost? Have you ever lost something dear to you—a favorite toy perhaps? Has someone you loved moved away? Discuss what it feels to experience a loss.
2. Jesus' simple explanation of being in his Father's house was enough for Mary, who "meek and obedient, was satisfied and did not ask for explanations" (page 43). How can you imitate this trait in your everyday life?
3. What words about Jesus and Mary would you like to keep in your heart?

Growing In Holiness

Just as journeying to the temple was a serious occasion to the Holy Family, so should be our journey to Mass to receive Jesus in the Holy Eucharist. Imitate the "solemnness" of the Holy Family as they made the journey to the temple. Maintan a holy silence as you travel to Mass. Use this time to enter into God's presence and to prepare your soul to receive our Lord and Savior.

📖 **Searching Scripture – Luke 2:41-52**

Each year his parents went to Jerusalem for the feast of Passover, and when he was twelve years old, they went up according to festival custom. After they had completed its days, as they were returning, the boy Jesus remained behind in Jerusalem, but his parents did not know it. Thinking that he was in the caravan, they journeyed for a day and looked for him among their relatives and acquaintances, but not finding him, they returned to Jerusalem to look for him. After three days they found him in the temple, sitting in the midst of the teachers, listening to them and asking them questions, and all who heard him were astounded at his understanding and his answers. When his parents saw him, they were astonished, and his mother said to him, "Son, why have you done this to us? Your father and I have been looking for you with great anxiety." And he said to them, "Why were you looking for me? Did you not know that I must be in my Father's house?" But they did not understand what he said to them. He went down with them and came to Nazareth, and was obedient to them; and his mother kept all these things in her heart. And Jesus advanced (in) wisdom and age and favor before God and man.

✓ **Checking the Catechism**

1. *What do you believe of Jesus Christ?* I believe that Jesus Christ is the Son of God, the second Person of the Blessed Trinity, true God and true man.
2. *Why is Jesus Christ true God?* Jesus Christ is true

God because He is the true and only Son of God the Father.

3. *Why is Jesus Christ true man?* Jesus Christ is true man because he is the Son of the Blessed Virgin Mary and has a body and soul like ours.

4. *How many natures are there is Jesus Christ?* In Jesus Christ there are two natures, the nature of God and the nature of man.

★REVIEW★ Adult Catechism

No. 87. Jesus is inseparably true God and true man. . . . As the Son of God . . . he was made true man, our brother, without ceasing to be God, our Lord. (See CCC No. 464-467 and 469.)

The Holy Family

Carina was most uncommonly thoughtful. There was almost a frown on her forehead, and her mouth was puckered into unnatural smallness. Of course, her mother saw, and was not at all astonished when the little daughter's perplexity found its voice at bedtime.

"Mommy, I've just got to tell you something about Amy and Daisy, it bothers me so," Carina declared.

"Does it? Well, you may always tell me everything. The only things mothers hate to hear are selfish little complaints and fault-finding."

Carina considered. Was this a complaint? No, she was really and truly troubled and doubtful, and at such times her mother even coaxed her worries into words.

"Amy and Daisy come over to play today," she began. "Mommy, is it true Amy is rich and Daisy is poor?"

"Why?" Mommy started. She hated to think Carina cared anything about money.

"Because," said Carina convincingly. That expression was a return to her very-little-baby days. It still slipped from her when she was greatly annoyed or interested. "Daisy went home first, Mommy, and afterwards Amy began to—to make comments—which wasn't nice, I know, Mommy, even if you didn't shake your head."

"But Carina might have changed the subject?" her mother hinted. "People aren't apt to persist in any particular style of conversation, dear, except we encourage them."

"I know," sighed Carina. "It's like you can't argue by yourself. But I got vexed, Mommy, and answered back, and so it just couldn't stop. Amy said Daisy's pants were hand-me-downs, and that Daisy's shirt was from last year, and—and—oh, yes, that her family was poor and didn't have a very nice house."

"What did you say, Carina?" seriously.

"I said I didn't care, and I loved Daisy, and it was not any disgrace to be poor." Her cheeks flushed.

"And then?"

"Amy said she couldn't stand to be poor, and her mother came that minute and she went home." Carina's face was full of trouble. She believed Amy had offended Daisy, and she loved Daisy dearly, and somehow Amy's view of the circumstances of Daisy's life was disappointing and hurt deep down in Carina's heart.

Several seconds were ticked away by the bedroom clock before Carina's mother spoke. Having told her woes, Carina rested comfortably upon the arm that held her and grew almost drowsy gazing into the darkening space.

"Carina," began Mommy at last, "who do you suppose was the truest lady the world ever saw?"

"You," she replied promptly and simply, her big eyes raised suddenly to her mother's own.

Her mother laughed, a tender laugh with a bit of sadness in it.

"Of me, darling, you aren't a fit judge. I don't mean anyone belonging to ordinary mortals like us, Carina. Think of somebody far above us."

"O—oh," Carina eagerly interrupted, "now I know! The Blessed Mother. You often call her 'our Lady.'"

"Certainly. Mary was the most perfect lady the world ever knew. No one has ever been, or ever will be, so gentle and refined as she. Neither was anyone ever so tender and sensitive. She was of royal blood, too; so, even in the estimation of worldly and material people, Mary was a lady born and bred. Who was her famous ancestor, Carina?"

"I forget, Mommy."

"Don't you remember how Mary was of the house of David? David was a great king, and Solomon, his son, was the king whom we call, above all others, 'the Wise Man.' In the Bible, he has left us a book known by the wonderful title of 'The Book of Wisdom.' Now Mary was of this royal house of David, the descendant of great kings, worthy of the state of a princess even from a simply human standpoint. She was beautiful, also, beyond any other of the children of men, and beauty seems to command service in this world of ours."

"She was 'all fair,'"[11] murmured Carina, as her mother paused.

"Yes; all fair. That means she was perfect. Now, besides the honor which her royal blood and her beauty and sweetness demanded, Mary's sanctity would seem to need a deeper homage yet. And still, that is not all."

"No," said Carina earnestly; "she was Jesus' mother besides, and that's why she was full of grace, and so beautiful, and God loved her so."

"My little girl understands very well. Imagine the Blessed Mother with her Son and St. Joseph, and tell me how they lived. Was it in wealth and luxury, Carina? How beautiful a house did Mary have?"

"Oh, Mommy!" breathed Carina, suddenly strangely ashamed.

"We know she didn't have a fancy house. St. Joseph was a carpenter, working hard at that simple trade. Jesus helped, and the Holy Family kept their home as plainly as their neighbors. Mary worked at the household tasks. She worked as your little friend's Amy's servants work—the greatest Lady who ever lived! In heaven the angels call her Queen, and rejoice to do her bidding; but at Nazareth she toiled at what many consider drudgery, and often her assistant was our Lord himself. He did not complain about helping her as many children do. You know the Gospel tells us how when Jesus and Mary and Joseph returned from Jerusalem after the finding in the temple, that Jesus was subject to Mary and Joseph.

---

[11] From the Litany of the Holy Name of Mary

That means that our dear Lord acted as their obedient and devoted child, doing in perfection every little service other loving children do the best they may."

"It's never perfect, is it, Mommy?" Carina asked, somewhat mischievously. How often, instead of helping, had her would-be assistance caused Mommy and Grandma merely additional trouble! "But I love to try to help anyway."

"I think all children do. And all mothers love the attempts small girls and boys make to be of use, darling. The good will counts for a great deal, and mistakes make little folks wiser the next time. Jesus made no mistakes. Eternal wisdom was always his possession, and in his loving services of his mother, he always knew exactly what would be best. But the household was not managed by miracles, Carina. We mustn't forget that the Holy Family labored the same way other poor people do. St. Joseph used his tools and kept his workshop in order, the holy Child aided him, and the Blessed Mother prepared the meals and mended clothes and cleaned the little house, Jesus in turn going to her assistance. The only difference their lives bore to those about them was the holiness which filled every action, performed as it was in the Real Presence of Jesus and very often with his visible bodily assistance."

"I wish," said 'Carina, "I'd been alive then, Mommy, and could have gone every day to call on the Blessed Mother and Baby Jesus."

"Lots of people have wished that, Carina. And still, if we had been upon the earth and in Nazareth while Jesus lived there, how can we know that we'd have been amongst Jesus' friends? Think of all who refused to believe in him, dear, and let us be glad we were born with the Faith as our inheritance. Hundreds passed him as a Child, perhaps carrying a jar of water for his mother or handling the carpenter's tools with St. Joseph, and did not recognize his divinity, although no doubt his smile and silent benediction brought to many the grace of conversion later.

"So the years passed in humble poverty and toil at Nazareth; no servants, Carina, no idleness, and no show of the glory which belonged to the Holy Family. Until Jesus was thirty years old, he lived that simple, quiet existence which we call 'The Hidden Life', in company with the Blessed Mother and St. Joseph. The angels of God gave them honor, but of human attendants to wait upon them there was not one.

"What do you think of Amy's remark now, darling? In the face of the work our Blessed Lady did?"

Dear little Carina gazed up at her mother, a deep, deep look in her eyes.

"'I'm sorry," said she simply, "that Amy doesn't know better."

Discussion Questions

1. Have you ever been guilty of sharing "selfish little complaints and fault-finding"? Discuss what

you can do to become more aware (and eliminate) this habit. What can you do to increase your gratitude toward God and become less judgmental of others?

2. Have you ever thought less of someone because of how they dressed or how much money they seemed to have? Have you ever been annoyed or jealous of someone who seems to have lots of money and "stuff"? How does realizing how very little the Holy Family had (and how simply they lived) change your ideas about being rich or poor?

3. What little acts of loving service can you perform for your family? Why it is important to always try to help around the house?

✠ Growing In Holiness

"The only difference their lives bore to those about them was the holiness which filled every action" (page 51). Every action done with love and cheerfulness, with the intention of pleasing God and pleasing others, is a holy action. Try to do everything you do—household chores, schoolwork, small favors for friends and neighbors—with love.

✓ Checking the Catechism

1. *What is the Tenth Commandment?* The Tenth Commandment is: You shall not covet your neighbor's goods.

2. *What are we commanded by the Tenth Commandment?* By the Tenth Commandment, we are com-

manded to be content with what we have, and to rejoice in our neightbor's welfare.

REVIEW **Adult Catechism**

No. 532. Jesus calls his disciples to prefer him to everything and everyone. Detachment from riches . . . free us from anxiety . . . and prepare us for [the kingdom of heaven]." (See CCC Nos. 2544-2547 and 2556.)

St. John the Baptist

He always interested Carina immensely. It was one of her earliest amusements of imagination to lay very still, her eyes tightly closed, and picture St. John in the desert wearing "clothing made of camel's hair and . . . a leather belt around his waist."[12]

There was another picture of St. John—a real picture, framed and hanging in her mother's room—of St. John as a little boy. Carina loved that, too. In it the Blessed Mother held the Infant Jesus on her lap, and St. John, looking upward, leaned against her knee.

"He is learning from Jesus," Carina once said to her mother.

"Yes," her mom had answered. "They were very near each other. St. John's mother, Elizabeth, was Mary's cousin. It was to the home of Elizabeth that the Blessed Virgin went after the archangel Gabriel announced to her that she would become the Mother of God. Mary stayed with Elizabeth for three months, and they loved each other dearly. About that time,

---

[12] Matthew 3:4

St. John was born, coming into the world six months before our Lord. You see, he was called the precursor, or forerunner, of Jesus. And just as his preaching began before that of Jesus, so his birth was before the advent of Christ."

"And St. John stayed years in the desert, Mommy?"

"Yes, living on locusts and wild honey."

Carina winced. As for eating locusts and wild honey, she assured her mother that no degree of hunger could force her to partake of the locusts.

"But they dry locusts in the East, dear, and so make them acceptable," her mother explained.

"Never mind," said Carina, firm in her opinion; "but, anyway, the wild honey must have been delicious." So in her imagination, Carina conscientiously remembered the locusts as in duty bound, but passed beyond them as quickly as possible and lingered long over the mantle of camel's hair and the delightful honey. Kingly figure was the St. John her imagination painted, a character quaintly symbolized by the strength of the animal that furnished his mantle and the sweetness of the honey which nourished him.

"He wasn't lonely in the desert, was he, Mommy? Because he could talk to God and the angels without anyone to interrupt him, and I suppose the bees buzzed as softly—" Carina dropped her eyelids and smiled at the sunlit peace of her dear St. John the Baptist. Suddenly, a doubt made her flash a quick glance up at her mother.

"But he wasn't the St. John called 'the beloved disciple,' Mommy?"

"No; St. John the Apostle is called 'the beloved disciple.' The Apostles were called during Christ's life; St. John the Baptist preached penance and baptized before Christ began his public life. Except the time he was three days in Jerusalem—when Mary and Joseph thought he was lost—Jesus lived a quiet life at home for thirty years. People believed him to be a simple carpenter, devoted to his parents and to his work with them. When Jesus was thirty years old, he left Nazareth and began his public life."

"How long was that, Mommy?"

"Well, you tell me. Jesus was crucified when he was thirty-three. How long, then, was he preaching?"

Carina beamed. That was easy. "Three years, Mommy."

"Exactly. And for some time before Jesus left Nazareth, St. John was preaching to crowds of people. The world was very wicked at that time."

"Worse than now?" queried Carina, astonished. Had not Grandma said that very morning, "I don't know what the world is coming to?"

"Very much worse, dear. Rome was heathen, and its wickedness had spread over all the land it governed. The Jews were constantly quarreling and at war among themselves, besides being affected by the manners of their Roman conquerors and the arrogance."

"What is that?" interrupted Carina.

Her mother smiled. "Pride, darling."

"Oh, I see," gravely; "stuck-up-ness."

Then Mommy laughed outright.

"That's an awful word, Carina, but it exactly expresses arrogance. The Pharisees thought they possessed everything, particularly religion, in a fuller and better degree than other people. They made a great fuss and show about the forms of religion, and lived far away from God so far as their hearts were concerned. They belonged to those people of whom Jesus said, 'This people honors me with their lips, but their hearts are far from me.'[13] So, when John the Baptist began to preach in the desert, he was facing hard conditions even amongst the Jews."

"And St. John scolded them awfully," said Carina, sitting up straight and frowning dramatically. "He saw them coming, those Pharisees and the other ones, Mommy—what do you call them?"

"Sadducees—they were another class of Jews. Go on, Carina; what did St. John say to the Pharisees and Sadducees when they went out to the desert to join the crowds of people who were listening to St. John's preaching?"

"'You brood of vipers! Who warned you to flee from the coming wrath?'"[14] Carina uttered the words in a very fierce tone.

"Yes, and by the 'coming wrath,' dear, is meant the anger of God. St. John knew the falseness and pretense of the Pharisees, and warned them to do penance and change the manner of their lives. He was, as he himself told the people, the man of whom the prophet wrote, 'A voice of one crying out in the

---

[13] Matthew 15:8
[14] Luke 3:7

desert, Prepare the way of the Lord, make straight his paths.'[15] He labored to have some souls ready for the coming of Jesus, and, indeed, many repented, confessed their sins, and were baptized.

"Now you may easily imagine, Carina, that no one could convert a great many people from evil to good, either in these days or in the time of St. John the Baptist, without starting a great deal of talk. This holy man, who had spent years alone in the desert, this man who spoke with authority and who dared reprimand even the proud, self-satisfied Pharisees, who could he be? As greater and greater crowds went out to him from Jerusalem and all the surrounding country, the priests' wonder grew and an anxious curiosity possessed them. Surely, it was time to find out what all this preaching and baptizing meant.

"So some of the priests and Levites finally went out from Jerusalem themselves and, going straight to St. John, they asked him. 'Who are you?'[16] They expected him to answer that he was Christ. But he told them distinctly, 'I am not the Messiah.'[17] This rather disappointed them, but they were not satisfied and continued to question, thinking St. John might claim to be Elijah. Imagine them waiting eagerly for his second answer, Carina, and their surprise when he again told them, 'I am not.'[18] Having learned nothing, they finally demanded plainly,

---

[15] Luke 3:4
[16] John 1:19
[17] John 1:20
[18] John 1:21

'Who are you?'[19] They were of the Pharisees and could not bear to return to Jerusalem humiliated by not succeeding in their mission. No doubt they had counted upon St. John's being confused and alarmed by their visit. Instead, he answered them as he had replied to the others: 'I am the voice of one cryingout in the desert.'[20] And when they wanted to know why he baptized, as he was neither Christ nor Elijah, he told them of the coming of Jesus: '. . . there is one among you whom you do not recognize, the one who is coming after me, whose sandal strap I am not worthy to untie.'[21] Beautiful words, aren't they?"

"Yes, Mommy. He loved Jesus."

"Surely. It seems to me that the Acts of Faith, Hope and Charity are all contained in those words, dear, and the Act of Humility besides. The next day came St. John's reward. Standing there by the Jordan, he saw Jesus coming—coming to him. And seeing him, St. John cried out the words every priest says before he gives Holy Communion to the people: 'Behold, the Lamb of God, who takes away the sins of the world.'[22]

"Then our dear Lord was baptized in the River Jordan by St. John. At first, St. John almost refused to baptize his Savior, but Jesus told him 'Allow it now, for thus it is fitting for us to fulfill all righteousness.'[23] What a privilege that baptism of the Son of

---

[19] John 1:22
[20] John 1:23
[21] John 1:26
[22] John 1:29b
[23] Matthew 3:15

God was to St. John, dear! And as he baptized, the heavens opened, and St. John saw the Holy Spirit in the form of a dove, descending upon Jesus. Then came a voice from heaven saying: 'This is my beloved Son, with whom I am well pleased.'[24] So were the Three Persons of the Blessed Trinity all represented at the baptism of Jesus."

"How, Mommy?" asked Carina, not quite comprehending.

"Jesus in his humanity, darling, the Holy Spirit in the form of a dove, and God the Father in the voice. Now, darling, it is very late, and our story has taken longer than usual. Does my little girl want to hear the rest?"

"Oh, yes, Mommy; I always love to hear about St. John the Baptist. Only"—regretfully—"I don't like the way he died."

"It was a martyrdom, Carina, a death for the teachings of Jesus. Herod, the king, was very wicked, and married the wife of his brother. St. John reproved him for this sin, and Herod, very angry, had him cast into prison. But this did not silence St. John. He would not take back the truth, and continued to say, 'It is not lawful that you should have her.'[25] However, Herod no longer bothered about St. John, having once put him into prison. But the wife, Herodias, was furious because St. John condemned her. And she took an awful revenge. You see, she could quiet her own conscience, but she could not prevent St. John from

---

[24] Matthew 3:17
[25] Matthew 14:4

declaring that she was committing a great sin. So she laid her plans to have Herod give the order that St. John should be beheaded. This Herodias had a pretty young daughter who danced very beautifully, and Herodias arranged for her to dance at Herod's birthday party. The king gave a great feast to celebrate the day, and after dinner, Herodias's daughter came in and danced. Herod was delighted. In his pleasure he bade her ask him anything, even to the half of his kingdom, and he would gladly grant her request."

"But he didn't know she'd ask anything about St. John."

"No, indeed. We are told that Herod's heart was sad when the young girl came back from her wicked mother and asked, in obedience to that mother, the head of St. John the Baptist. The king was astonished and shocked. But he was weak, and terribly influenced by human respect."

"What is that, Mommy?"

"The fear of what people will say—of public opinion. It is putting the opinions of foolish sinners like ourselves ahead of God's law. So Herod, as the Bible says, 'because of . . . the guests who were present,'[26] as well as because of his oath to the damsel, sent to the prison and had St. John beheaded. A dreadful death, Carina, if we consider it in a weak, human way, but a glorious death for Jesus and his teaching, when we look at it in the light of our holy Faith."

"Yes," said Carina, a few tears shining in her

---

[26] Matthew 14:9

eyes; "St. John lived for Jesus, so he didn't mind dying for him. Goodnight, Mommy dear, and thank you."

Discussion Questions

1. What do you like best about St. John the Baptist? In what ways can you imitate him? In what ways would it be hard?
2. Carina says that St. John the Baptist loved Jesus. What do you do to show Jesus that you love him? Can others tell by your words and actions that you love Jesus? Name at least three people that you know that love Jesus. How can you tell?
3. Discuss what it means to be "influenced by human respect." Think of times when you have been more worried about what your friends will say instead of considering whether or not you are offending God. Consider this weakness when you make your nightly examination of conscience.

Growing In Holiness

Maybe you can't live on wild honey and locusts, or dress in itchy camel's hair, but you can do penance and make sacrifices for Jesus. Consider at least one thing that you can give up and one thing that you can do (or eat) that you don't like. Try to do at least one of these things each day for Jesus in imitation of St. John the Baptist.

▥ Searching Scripture – Matthew 3:1-12

In those days John the Baptist appeared, preaching in the desert of Judea (and) saying, "Repent, for the Kingdom of Heaven is at hand!" It was of him that the prophet Isaiah had spoken when he said:

"A voice of one crying out in the desert,
'Prepare the way of the Lord,
  make straight his paths.'"

John wore clothing made of camel's hair and had a leather belt around his waist. His food was locusts and wild honey. At that time Jerusalem, all Judea, and the whole region around the Jordan were going out to him and were being baptized by him in the Jordan River as they acknowledged their sins.

When he saw many of the Pharisees and Sadducees coming to his baptism, he said to them, "You brood of vipers! Who warned you to flee from the coming wrath? Produce good fruit as evidence of your repentance. And do not presume to say to yourselves, 'We have Abraham as our father.' For I tell you, God can raise up children to Abraham from these stones. Even now the ax lies at the root of the trees. Therefore every tree that does not bear good fruit will be cut down and thrown into the fire. I am baptizing you with water, for repentance, but the one who is coming after me is mightier than I. I am not worthy to carry his sandals. He will baptize you with the holy Spirit and fire. His winnowing fan is in his hand. He will clear his threshing floor and gather his wheat into his barn, but the chaff he will burn with unquenchable fire."

St. John the Baptist

(If desired, read Matthew 14:3-12, which describes
Herod's promise to the daughter of Herodias and the
consequences to St. John the Baptist as described
above.)

✓ **Checking the Catechism**

1. *What is contrition, or sorrow for sin?* Contrition,
   or sorrow for sin, is a hatred of sin and a true
   grief of the soul for having offended God, with a
   firm purpose of sinning no more.
2. *Why should we be sorry for our sins?* We should
   be sorry for our sins, because sin is the greatest
   of evils and an offense against God our Creator,
   Preserver, and Redeemer, and because it shuts
   us out of heaven and condemns us to the eternal
   pains of hell.
3. *What is Baptism?* Baptism is a sacrament which
   cleanses us from original sin, makes us Chritians,
   children of God, and heirs of heaven.
4. *Is Baptism necessary to salvation?* Baptism is necessary to salvation, because without it we cannot
   enter into the Kindgom of Heaven.

REVIEW Adult Catechism

No. 261. Baptism is necessary for salvation for all
those to whom the Gospel has been proclaimed and
who have had the possibility of asking for this sacrament. (See CCC No. 1257.)

The Forty Days' Fast

"How many days in a month, Mommy?" queried Carina.

"Thirty-one in most, dear; but April, June, September and November have only thirty—"

"And February twenty-eight, except in leap year, when it has 'one day more,'" quoted Carina, the time-worn rhyme coming back to her memory. "Then, Mommy, Jesus fasted more than a whole month, didn't he?"

"Yes—a whole month of thirty days, and ten days more."

"It was a very long time," said Carina gravely, "and Jesus must have been very, very hungry."

"He was, and we are expressly told how Satan knew he was hungry and so first tempted him through this hunger. The divinity of Jesus had been proclaimed in a special manner just before the long fast of our Lord. You know Jesus was baptized in the River Jordan by St. John, and many miracles occurred at that time: the heavens were opened; the Holy Spirit descended in the form of a dove; and a voice from heaven uttered those wonderful words: 'This is my beloved Son, with whom I am well pleased.'[27] All these circumstances attended the baptism of Jesus to show forth his divinity. Then he went to the desert, to fast as the man, to be tired and weak and hungry, as you and I and all human creatures can be."

"And it's very uncomfortable," declared Carina.

"It most certainly is. And if we are suffering for the want of food, Carina, it is very hard indeed to restrain the natural impulse to take the first food we see."

"Yes," sighed the little girl; "it was awfully hard to be hungry after I had scarlet fever and the doctor would not let me eat. Once, Mommy—" Carina paused, flushing all over her chubby face and neck.

"Well?"

"Once—I nearly got out of bed to sneak a piece of cake." The confession was out, and Carina hid her face, as relieved as she was ashamed.

"But you didn't, darling. The temptation was there, but you didn't give in, and that will always stand to your credit. Don't you see? God never forgets anything. He will always remember my little girl resisted when she really very badly wanted something good to eat. We're all tempted one way or another— you by the cake, and somebody else to vanity, and still another to anger, and so on; but the temptation is no sin. We never need yield, Carina—don't forget that. We always have power to say 'I will' or 'I won't'; and what we say settles the matter on the side of

---

[27] Matthew 3:17

68

our dear Lord, or directly against him, on the side of Satan."

"Sometimes it's 'I will,'" said Carina, "and other times it's 'I won't.' If it's my morning prayer I don't feel like saying, Mommy, then I've just got to say 'I will,' and if I feel awfully like disobeying you, I've got to say 'I won't.'"

"Quite so. Now don't get them mixed, Carina, and say 'I will' at the wrong time," her mother laughed. "Only hold bravely to the knowledge that no power can force you to do wrong, either in a small matter or a great, big one. It's a cheerful thought, Carina, and our Lord loves us to have cheerful thoughts. He gives us his grace—or his help, which word you better understand—to choose the right, provided we accept it. He never fails, although we do. And so, sure of his grace—or help—he tells us 'Rejoice and be glad'[28]—'. . . no one will take your joy away from you'[29]—he wants us to be happy, Carina."

"I like to be happy, Mommy, but I can't when I'm disappointed, or people are horrid, or I hurt myself."

"You can't be happy and carefree always, darling, that is true; but you can be at peace, and that is real happiness. You know that God will reward you for everything—no matter how small—you do or suffer for him, and you know that heaven is waiting for you. Isn't heaven cheap at any price, Carina?"

"Yes, Mommy. Because it will never stop."

"Exactly. After all our trials comes heaven. Just

---

[28] Matthew 5:12

[29] John 16:22b

as after Jesus had passed through temptations, the angels came and ministered to him. The first temptation appealed to his exceeding hunger: Satan offered Jesus stones, saying: '. . . command that these stones become loaves of bread.'[30] But Jesus, weak and fasting in his humanity, was almighty in his divinity, and answered Satan: 'One does not live by bread alone, but by every word that comes forth from the mouth of God.'[31]

"Still Satan did not give up. Jesus could overcome his hunger; Satan, whose own pride had cast him into hell, would tempt our Lord by pride. Accordingly, he took Jesus into Jerusalem and set him upon the pinnacle of the temple. Seeing him there, Satan cried, 'If you are the Son of God, throw yourself down. For it is written: 'He will command his angels concerning you and with their hands they will support you, lest you dash your foot against a stone.'[32] And Jesus, poised between heaven and earth, answered in all tranquility, 'You shall not put the Lord, your God, to the test.'[33]

"Now Satan had kept his strongest temptation for the last. He often does that, little one. First a tiny thing tempts us—so trifling that sometimes we see no danger at all. The second time the temptation is more serious, and at last comes one which almost conquers us. Having completely failed with our dear Lord, Satan presented the temptation which has

---

[30] Matthew 4:3
[31] Matthew 4:4
[32] Matthew 4:6
[33] Matthew 4:7

ruined the happiness of many a soul. He took Jesus up into a high mountain and showed him all the kingdoms of the world, and the beauty and glory and riches of them."

"The whole world at once, Mommy?" wide-eyed.

"Yes, dear. The sea with its ships and its treasures, the land with its cities and forests and fertile fields, gold and jewels and precious stuffs, besides millions of human beings. Satan offered the service and homage of all these, and the glory they would bring, to Jesus—in the eyes of the world the poor carpenter of Nazareth. And at what price? See, Carina, how, in exchange for all this, Satan wished to be adored in place of God himself. It very often happens to people that they worship money and worldly honor instead of God; in other words, they make idols of wealth and pleasure and advancement. Forgetting God, they sacrifice faith and honesty and justice to become rich, to get ahead in the world. So they worship idols, because anything put into the place belonging to God above becomes an idol."

"Does it, Mommy?" surprised. "Why, I thought an idol had to be a graven image."

"No, indeed. Some idols are cut out of stone or wood, to be sure, but we can make an idol of anything. Even"—and here Mommy hugged her small daughter closely—"of a little girl like you, if we love her more than we love God. Well, where were we? Oh, yes; Satan asked Jesus to adore him, in return for the gift of the whole world. But our Blessed Lord said, 'The Lord, your God, shall you worship and him alone shall you serve.'[34]

"Then the devil left Jesus, God's grace having triumphed. And the heavenly Father sent his angels to his beloved Son, and they ministered to him. That is the way it is always, Carina, even with us poor sinners; after trials and temptations, come the angels of God to console us. As certainly as the sunshine follows the rain, does the light of comfort visit us after the darkness and doubt of trouble."

"But I never have the darkness and doubt," protested Carina sleepily. "I'm very happy, Mommy."

"Yes, dear. God bless you!" And Mommy laid her down.

Discussion Questions

1. Honestly share some of your temptations. Discuss ways you can resist these temptations. How can we avoid those situations that put us in temptation? How can we support each other in resisting temptation?

2. Do you believe that heaven is "cheap at any price"? What does this mean? What are you willing to sacrifice to get to heaven?

3. In what ways have you made idols of money and worldly honor? When do things of this world come before God in your life? Do you care more about what other people think of you than offending God?

---

[34] Matthew 4:10

✝ Growing In Holiness

In Matthew 6—after Jesus tells us to be perfect as God is perfect—he gives us the three-ply cord (Ecclesiastes 4:12) of Christian duty; he tells us how to give, how to pray, and how to fast. The powerful spiritual tool of fasting has fallen out of favor with many people. (When is the last time *you* fasted?) Consider how to incorporate fasting into your spiritual life (give up a specific meal a day for a week, give up a specific food or a time-wasting habit). See how God rewards you!

📖 Searching Scripture – Matthew 4:1-11

Then Jesus was led by the Spirit into the desert to be tempted by the devil. He fasted for forty days and forty nights, and afterwards he was hungry. The tempter approached and said to him, "If you are the Son of God, command that these stones become loaves of bread." He said in reply, "It is written:

'One does not live by bread alone,
    but by every word that comes forth
        from the mouth of God.'"

Then the devil took him to the holy city, and made him stand on the parapet of the temple, and said to him, "If you are the Son of God, throw yourself down. For it is written:

'He will command his angels concerning you
    and 'with their hands they will support you,
        lest you dash your foot against a stone.'"

Jesus answered him, "Again it is written, 'You shall not put the Lord, your God, to the test.'" Then the devil took him up to a very high mountain, and showed him all the kingdoms of the world in their magnificence, and he said to him, "All these I shall give to you, if you will prostrate yourself and worship me." At this, Jesus said to him, "Get away, Satan! It is written:

'The Lord, your God, shall you worship
and him alone shall you serve.'"

Then the devil left him and, behold, angels came and ministered to him.

✓ Checking the Catechism

1. *What is actual grace?* Actual grace is that help of God which enlightens our mind and moves our will to shun evil and do good.

2. *Does God reward anything but our good works?* God rewards our good intention and desire to serve Him, even when our works are not successful. We should make this good intention often during the day, and especially in the morning.

3. *What is the best means of overcoming temptation?* The best means of overcoming temptation is to resist its very beginning, by turning our attention from it; by praying for help to resist it; and by doing the opposite of what we are tempted to do.

✶REVIEW✶ Adult Catechism

No. 496. [In the Our Father], we ask God . . . not to leave us alone and in the power of temptation. We ask the Holy Spirit to help us know how to discern . . . between a *trial* that makes us grow in goodness and a *temptation* that leads to sin and death . . . (See CCC Nos. 2846-2849 and 2863.)

Calling the Apostles

Sometimes it was very hard for Carina to answer, even at home in the city; but when Carina was in the woody, hilly, beautiful country, where the brooks gurgled lovingly and the shy, pretty birds stole inquisitive glances at her golden head from the trees, "Carina, Carina!" could echo several times through the silence before the willful little person would call, "Yes, Mommy; I'm coming."

"Oh dear!" sighed Carina at last. Then she sent a rather cross, "I'm coming," through the trees and gathered up her toys.

Carina did not forget this act of disobedience. That night, when Mommy came into the bedroom to tuck her in, it was just as if that bubbling, busybody brook came into the room, too, and gurgled: "Naughty Carina! She heard and she wouldn't answer. She didn't want to come!"

Carina closed her eyes, drew a long breath and, reaching for Mommy's hand, whispered hastily, "I heard you calling for ever so long this afternoon, Mommy; and I didn't want to come!"

Her eyes opened suddenly to see how Mommy

would look. But Mommy's other hand hid Mommy's face.

"I knew you heard," said Mommy; "I was only wondering how long my little girl would take to answer."

When Mommy stopped speaking, the bedroom clock ticked a great many seconds away before Carina at length broke the stillness. An easily-recognized defiance touched the sleepy voice into wakeful clearness: "I don't like to be obedient." Carina stared steadily into the twilight, away from Mommy's gaze.

"It's funny, Carina, almost nobody likes to be obedient; many people hate to be so." One of Mommy's sly little laughs rippled close to Carina's ear. "Especially little people with great, big, strong wills of their own."

"I don't like to be called when I'm playing," Carina went on, but more meekly. "I can't bear to stop, and it seems to me, Mommy," Carina paused, a bit afraid.

"Go on, little one," Mommy encouraged.

"It's not polite," Carina explained anxiously.

"Never mind. Tell me just what you were thinking."

"Well—if you'd wait, Mommy, till I'd finished, I'd not mind answering and coming then."

"That wouldn't be obedience, dear. It would be exactly the opposite: doing your own will instead of somebody else's. Can't you see that?"

Carina considered. She was really not anxious to see. Carina did hate to give in. Something kept her tongue from moving whenever it was necessary to say she had been mistaken about anything.

"Obedience is something God loves very much," Mommy went on, passing over Carina's unwillingness to speak. "The Child Jesus was subject to the Blessed Mother and St. Joseph; which means Jesus obeyed them. And when he had grown to manhood, the Bible tells us he became obedient unto the death of the Cross. That means Jesus obeyed the will of his heavenly Father to the very end of his life. And what was the end, Carina?"

"The Crucifixion," said Carina, promptly but slowly; for Mommy liked words pronounced clearly and that word was a hard one for Carina.

"That was the way Jesus showed his obedience, which ended only on the Cross. The proof of our obedience never reaches such a price. But, daughter, while so little is asked of us, let us at least answer if we're called."

"Yes, Mommy," said Carina, suddenly ashamed. "I'm sorry," she added quickly.

"We'll take the twelve Apostles for our story tonight. Jesus called and they answered, and by his help they taught the Gospel to the world, the big world, stretching out into thousands of miles."

"Only twelve," said Carina wonderingly.

"Only twelve," Mommy repeated, "but twelve obedient and faithful unto death."

"They followed Jesus," said the child, "and so they learned from him."

"And what they learned from him they taught the world, the world of their own time, and all who came after them, down to you and me, Carina."

"Such a long, long time, and such millions of people!" Carina sighed.

"Nearly two thousand years, and many, many millions of people, believing with the same faith Christ taught his Apostles. Suppose, Carina, when Jesus called they had not answered? Then Jesus would have called others and those twelve could never have been Apostles. If they refused to answer the Master when he spoke to them, perhaps they would have been among the very people who cried, 'Let him be crucified!'[35] on Good Friday. Some people Jesus calls only once. If they remain silent, or say, 'I will not come', they are not again offered a chance. We know there was one rich man whom Jesus called and who refused to come. Our Lord did not ask him again.[36] But let us see what the twelve Apostles did. Do you know who was called first, Carina?"

"I think it was St. Peter," a little uncertainly.

"Yes; St. Peter is the one we speak of as Prince of the Apostles. He was the first pope, and it was God's will to call him first. But with St. Peter, Jesus called Andrew, his brother. They were busy fishermen, who worked hard to earn their living. It was not from play they were called, Carina.

"One day our Lord was teaching the people, and the crowds were so great on the shore that he went into Peter's boat and taught them out of it. When he had finished the sermon, Jesus commanded them to start again and let down their nets. Then St. Peter

[35] Matthew 27:22b
[36] See Luke 18:18-23.

answered: 'Master, we have worked hard all night and have caught nothing, but at your command I will lower the nets.'[37] Wasn't that perfect faith? Although the sun had risen and the natural time for fishing was past, although to human minds it would seem foolish and unreasonable to attempt in the daylight what had been impossible through the night, at the word of Jesus without a question Peter and Andrew once more cast their nets into the sea. With God, nothing is impossible.

"Presently, the nets grew heavy; they dragged almost beyond the control of the two fishermen, who were not prepared for the immense weight and strain. Can't you see them, Carina, tugging at the ropes, breathless and eager and totally astonished? In a moment, the great miraculous draught seemed slipping from them, and very much alarmed they shouted to James and John, two of their friends, to come help them land the multitude of fish into the boat. Amazed, even terrified, St. Peter looked at the shining fish in the nets. Never before had he seen so many. Speechless, Andrew and James and John stood by wondering who Jesus was, that at his word the sea gave up its treasures. But St. Peter recognized the power of God, and falling to his knees in adoration and humility, he cried out, 'Depart from me, Lord, for I am a sinful man.'"[38]

"And did Jesus leave poor St. Peter?" asked Carina. "I'd have prayed, 'Please don't go away, dear Jesus!'"

---

[37] Luke 5:5
[38] Luke 5:8b

"St. Peter recognized his unworthiness, dear, as even the holiest must in the presence of God. And Jesus spoke to him with loving gentleness: 'Do not be afraid; from now on you will be catching men.'[39] Wonderful as the draught of fish was, it was only a faint picture of the success which was to follow the preaching of the Gospel. St. Peter and the other Apostles were to win countless souls from wickedness to the service of God. At the word of Jesus, the net was filled, and through the Gospel, which is God's word to the whole world, heaven will be filled. Even a wee girl like Carina can understand how truly the Apostles became—as Jesus had foretold—'fishers of men.'[40]

"So they followed him, Peter, and Andrew, his brother, and James and John, the sons of Zebedee. They left all things; they didn't say, 'Who will provide for us?' nor 'Where shall we leave our nets?' nor 'Let's finish first what we like to do.' The Master called and they went instantly in simple obedience, as Jesus likes all his followers to do. Do you suppose it was easy to obey, Carina?"

"I don't know, Mommy. I suppose it was for them," doubtfully.

"It surely wasn't easy to their human nature, dear. They left their houses, their families, people they liked, even the fish they had just taken from the sea, without a question. It was the same with all the twelve. 'Follow me.'[41] Christ said, and 'they left

---

[39] Luke 5:10b
[40] Matthew 4:19b
[41] Luke 5:27b

everything and followed him.'[42] Philip, Matthew 'sitting at the customs post,'[43] Bartholomew, Thomas, the other James, Thaddeus, Simon, and Judas Iscariot, the traitor."

"Even Judas?" asked Carina, for she suddenly thought of that "human nature" that kept her tongue silent and her feet stubbornly still so often, and it seemed to her that Judas must have had a fearful amount of dreadful human nature.

"Yes, even Judas. He was called to be a great Apostle like the rest, and he went and followed Jesus at first. But gradually he grew careless, then his zeal and love died out, and finally he fell away, to commit the most awful sin the world ever saw. Judas did not persevere. Do you know what that means, Carina?"

"Kind of, Mommy."

"To persevere is to keep right on, not to forget our resolutions, or neglect them, not to go with Jesus one day and leave him the next."

"Then," said Carina very seriously, "it's being stubborn the right way. I like to persevere—being naughty. If I did exactly the same, kept straight on being good, Mommy, and—and came as soon as I was called and obeyed everything you said, would that be persevering?"

"Surely, Carina—persevering in your little-girl way as all the twelve except Judas persevered to be the Apostles of our holy Faith. Keep right on, brave and happy and patient, and who knows what call

[42] Luke 5:11b
[43] Luke 5:27

may come when Carina has grown up to be a strong woman? Our Lord had many disciples, people who learned of him, served him and did his will, people he dearly loved. But out of the multitude he chose only twelve to be Apostles. Before you fall asleep, let's say the Apostles' Creed, praying that we may always generously answer every call Jesus sends us."

Carina's drowsy voice began: "I believe . . ."

Discussion Questions

1. In what situations is obedience hardest for you? Do you think Jesus' obedience to the Father—the obedience that lead to his death on the Cross—was easy? What can you do to make obedience easier next time?
2. Why is it important in the spiritual life to do those things that are hard? What can we do to strengthen our will to do them?
3. What does it mean to "follow Jesus"? Name several times and circumstances in which Jesus has called you. How did you respond?

Growing In Holiness

To persevere is to "keep right on, not to forget our resolutions, or neglect them, not to go with Jesus one day and leave him the next" (page 81). List several resolutions about following Jesus that you think are important. Be faithful in keeping these resolutions.

📖 Searching Scripture – Matthew 4:18-22

As he was walking by the Sea of Galilee, he saw two brothers, Simon who is called Peter, and his brother Andrew, casting a net into the sea; they were fishermen. He said to them, "Come after me, and I will make you fishers of men." At once they left their nets and followed him. He walked along from there and saw two other brothers, James, the son of Zebedee, and his brother John. They were in a boat, with their father Zebedee, mending their nets. He called them, and immediately they left their boat and their father and followed him.

You may also wish to read Luke 5:1-11, "The Call of Simon the Fisherman."

✓ Checking the Catechism

1. *What is the grace of perseverance?* The grace of perseverance is a particular gift of God which enables us to continue in the state of grace till death.
2. *What does the gift of fortitude do?* The gift of fortitude disposes us to do what is good in spite of any difficulty.

🔺REVIEW🔺 Adult Catechism

No. 434. To the young man who asked this question ["What good must I do to have eternal life" (Matthew 19:16)], Jesus answered, "If you would enter into life, keep the commandments," and then he added, "Come, follow Me" (Matthew 19:16-21). To follow Jesus involves keeping the commandments. (See CCC Nos. 2052-2054 and 2075-2076.)

The Marriage at Cana

If ever a little girl was shining with happiness, Carina was, the day Aunt Grace was married. A wedding, a real bride in a long white train and a veil like a fairy cloud, with a flower wreath and a very big bouquet of the sweetest lilies; a procession up the wide church-aisle while the organ played and little boys sang; best of all, Carina herself walking ahead of Aunt Grace, strewing blossoms for the pretty white slippers to tread on, and every little while turning a broadly-smiling face around to peep at Aunt Grace's drooping head, and almost crying out, "Isn't she pretty?"

It was so lovely Carina never forgot it; and for the longest while she spoke of the occasion as her wedding. Of course, she stood very close to Aunt Grace and her groom Jack, and smiled at both with affectionate delight. Once she did something not entirely expected; when Aunt Grace was ready to have the bright wedding ring slipped upon her finger, Carina thought she did not see the small, eager niece waiting to take the beautiful bouquet.

"I'm here," said Carina cheerfully; "give it to me, Aunt Grace!"

But nobody minded really; a tiny indulgent smile pulled at the groom's lips and Uncle Jack—after the wedding he actually was Carina's Uncle Jack—whispered "Bless her!" under his breath.

Late in the afternoon, Aunt Grace and Uncle Jack went away, and soon afterward the very tired little girl drove home with her father and mother.

"There is, in fact, something intensely beautiful and solemn in a Catholic marriage," said Daddy.

Carina was only half listening; but when Mommy said "Yes; I was thinking all through the Mass of the two guests who were surely invited to this wedding, as they were to the marriage in Cana of Galilee," Carina suddenly sat up straight and blinked her heavy eyes into bright attention.

"Which two, Mommy?" she inquired very curiously.

"Jesus and Mary, dear."

"Oh!" said Carina, smiling with satisfaction. "We were very close to the tabernacle, Mommy, and I whispered a lot to Jesus about Aunt Grace."

"I'm glad you did," said Mommy, softly.

"But what was it about Cana?" Carina went on presently. "Is it a story? And will you tell it to me tonight?"

"Surely." And her mother did. It was the story she herself liked best just then.

"There was a marriage in Cana of Galilee," began Mommy, "and the mother of Jesus was there. Jesus also was invited, and his disciples, to the marriage.

We mustn't forget, Carina, how Jesus and Mary took part in the life about them. They did not despise nor ignore their neighbors; they did not refuse to bestow the simple, sweet little favors of life in the world. They made and received visits, they served and consoled all, they blessed and made happy by the humblest attentions everyone who came near them.

"Now there was to be a wedding in Cana, an event of joy, feasting, and congratulation. Some think the bridegroom was Nathaniel, the Israelite Jesus described as one in whom there was no guile, and one whom the Master certainly loved in a special way. Jesus and Mary knew the families of bride and groom, and like many others they were invited to the celebration of the marriage."

"They were a lucky bride and groom," said Carina. "I wish Aunt Grace had been alive then, and Uncle Jack, and I, and—" Carina paused, confused by the large number of people necessary to complete the wedding in her mind.

"Well, Aunt Grace and the rest of us weren't on earth when that particular marriage took place in Cana of Galilee, but Jesus and Mary are living now, and in heaven are as able and willing to help us, dear, as they were to help their friends while living in the world. We know our Lord was with us this morning, and I'm sure that the Blessed Mother was, too— Aunt Grace is a very devoted child of hers."

"Mothers don't leave their children," said Carina wisely, holding Mommy's hand close to one warm cheek, "and Mary is our mother."

"Yes, as tender and as loving as at Cana. The Jews celebrated weddings by a grand feast, a big party with lots to eat, and a great deal of wine. Now when a couple of hours had passed, Mary suddenly saw that all the wine had been drunk, and that the hosts and servants were embarrassed, not knowing what to do. There was no use asking the master of the house, for there was positively no more wine in the place, and the guests were waiting, thirsty and impatient. It was very uncomfortable, Carina, very mortifying to the host and very annoying that upon the special occasion of a wedding, he should not have enough wine for the guests.

"Then quietly and gently, in her own motherly dignity, Mary went to her divine Son. Very simply, she made known her wish to him, by saying 'They have no wine.'[44] She was sorry for the embarrassment of the good people, and she understood the power of our Lord. Besides, Mary knew how Jesus loved her, his dear mother; because of that love, he could not refuse nor disappoint her."

"But sometimes," said Carina with painful truthfulness, "I disappoint my mother, and yet I do love you."

"Certainly—only my little girl is a human being and nothing more, while the Blessed Mother's Child is human like ourselves and divine as God is, too. So we keep on trying to be like Jesus, and still we always must fall short of our model because we are

---

[44] John 2:3b

poor creatures striving to follow the Almighty Creator. Our Lord never did and never will refuse anything to his mother. When Mary went to him about that wine at the wedding feast, he told her the time for his miracles had not arrived. But her prayer was not left unanswered. Sure of her Son's power and mercy, Mary turned to the waiters, saying: 'Do whatever he tells you.'"[45]

"Mothers always know what to do," said Carina gravely.

"Good mothers try to do what is best, and Mary was the most perfect mother of the entire world. At her suggestion, Jesus commanded the waiters who were standing near six water pots of stone. You see, Carina, although our Lord's public life had but just begun, to please that dear mother he performed his first miracle then and there at the wedding feast in Cana.

"'Fill the jars with water,'[46] Jesus said, and without a question the waiters filled them to the brim. Then Jesus told them to draw out and carry to the chief steward of the feast, who was astonished to find wine instead of water in the jars. Hardly daring to believe what his eyes told him, the chief steward tasted the wine. Having tasted, he could no longer doubt, but in astonishment he called out to the bridegroom, asking why he had saved the finest wine till the very end of the feast. At all the feasts the steward had managed, people served the best wine first. He

---

[45] John 2:5
[46] John 2:7

could not understand why this bridegroom had kept the good wine for the last. The steward grew quite excited at such a new fashion of arranging things."

"He was silly," said Carina, "because whatever Jesus does is always right, isn't it, Mommy?"

"Of course. But the steward did not know of the miracle yet. It was the waiter who at once began to tell and explain how Jesus of Nazareth had turned the water into wine at his mother's request. In a moment, everyone knew of the wonderful act Jesus had done and praised and marveled at the power of the gentle guest. The disciples, who were at the wedding, believed in him more perfectly than before and joyously spread the power of his glory among the others. Jesus had shown his divinity, his complete power over everything seen and unseen, by changing the ordinary water into rich wine. We like to believe, Carina, that this first miracle, this raising of a common thing into something precious by our Lord, was the sign of the changing of marriage from a plain contract, or simple agreement, into one of the sacraments. Jesus worked the miracle of Cana because of his Blessed Mother's prayer. Perhaps, dear little girl, it was Mary's request which caused Jesus to make marriage a sacrament.

"I am sure, dear, that the bride and bridegroom thanked Jesus for the gift of the wine, and that the Blessed Mother did also. That is the way it always appears to me if we ask for anything through Mary's influence with her divine Son—that she thanks him for us after the favor is granted and I hope her gratitude atones a little bit for the poorness of our own. It is only to be expected that a mother will try to improve and make right what her children have tried to do, and the mother of Jesus is our mother, too."

"Like you take out the crooked stitches in my sewing," breathed Carina, "and the knots from the thread, and the blots one day I tried to write with ink; it was too hard," sighing sleepily.

The silence grew. Mommy was slipping away when the little girl roused herself to murmur, "It was a beautiful wedding, like Cana in Galilee, and Jesus was there."

Discussion Questions

1. Do you ever turn to Mary to ask for her help? What can she help you do today? What can she do for those you love? Remember to ask for her help often.
2. Carina tells her mother, "Whatever Jesus does is always right." Name some things Jesus has done for you in your life. Think of all the good things that have happened to you and all your blessings. What would you like to say to Jesus right now as you think of his loving action in your life?
3. Jesus showed his concern for his friends at the wedding in Cana by changing water into wine. Although we may never see a miracle like this in our daily lives, we know that he does shower his

grace upon us daily. What can you do to increase your awareness of God's care for you? What can you do to see his hand in all the minor details of daily living?

✝ Growing In Holiness

God is all around us, all the time, sharing in the emotions of our everyday life. Just as Carina and her family knew that Jesus and his mother were at Aunt Grace's wedding, so do we know that Jesus and Mary share in the all events of our day. Remember that Jesus walks with us each moment. Try to picture him alongside you as you move throughout your daily activities. Remember to talk with him. Try to become more aware of his presence.

📖 Searching Scripture – John 2:1-11

On the third day there was a wedding in Cana in Galilee, and the mother of Jesus was there. Jesus and his disciples were also invited to the wedding. When the wine ran short, the mother of Jesus said to him, "They have no wine." (And) Jesus said to her, "Woman, how does your concern affect me? My hour has not yet come." His mother said to the servers, "Do whatever he tells you." Now there were six stone water jars there for Jewish ceremonial washings, each holding twenty to thirty gallons. Jesus told them, "Fill the jars with water." So they filled them to the brim. Then he told them, "Draw some out now and take it to the headwaiter." So they took it. And when the headwaiter tasted the water that had become wine, without knowing where it came from (although the servers who had drawn the water knew), the headwaiter called the bridegroom and said to him, "Everyone serves good wine first, and then when people have drunk freely, an inferior one; but you have kept the good wine until now." Jesus did this as the beginning of his signs in Cana in Galilee and so revealed his glory, and his disciples began to believe in him.

✓ Checking the Catechism

1. *Does God see us?* God sees us and watches over us with loving care.
2. *What is God's loving care for us called?* God's loving care for us is called Divine Providence.
3. *What is the Sacrament of Matrimony?* The Sacrament of Matrimony is the sacrament that unites a Christian man and woman in lawful marriage.
4. *Can the bond of Christian marriage be dissolved by any human power?* The bond of Christian marriage cannot be dissolved by any human power.

✸REVIEW✸ Adult Catechism

No. 341. Christ not only restored the original order of matrimony but raised it to the dignity of a sacrament, giving spouses a special grace to live out their marriage as a symbol of Christ's love for his bride the Church . . . (See CCC Nos. 1612-1617and 1661.)

Jesus' Invitation to the Little Ones

"I know which story I'd like best tonight, Mommy," said Carina, climbing up into her mother's lap and kneeling there. The little face was flushed and half tearful and Mommy knew at once that everything had not been smooth and sunny with Carina that day.

"Which one, darling?" asked Mommy, curious to hear what Carina's choice would be.

"I think," said Carina very seriously, "I'd rather hear about the time Jesus was so tired, and still he said the children didn't bother him."

Mommy laughed a bit.

"Why that particular story, Carina?" The little girl hid her face against her mother's shoulder and did not answer at once.

"Has someone been bothered with my little daughter today? Some grown-up?"

"Yes, Mommy," Carina answered, sighing the biggest land of a sigh; "I won't say who, because you don't like tales. But someone was busy, and tired, too, I suppose, and she wasn't like Jesus, Mommy; she said, 'Don't bother me now; run away.'"

Mommy kissed the rosy cheek and stroked the curls back from Carina's forehead.

"You are quite right, darling: Jesus is never too busy for you, or for me, or for anyone in all the wide world."

"Yes, Mommy," settling herself comfortably in her mother's arms; "and please tell me all about it. How the disciples wouldn't have let the children come, and the mothers would have gone away."

"Very well, little one. It was one evening after Jesus had been preaching all day, telling people what was right and what was wrong, what pleased him and what displeased him, and our blessed Lord was very tired. You see, Jesus was human as well as divine, which means he was man as well as God, and so he suffered from cold and heat, and hunger and weariness, the same as we do. You know he had made the journey from Galilee to Judea, with crowds and crowds of people following him."

"In their cars, Mommy?"

"Oh, no, dear; there were no cars till nearly two thousand years later. We must think they went on foot, and the long way had helped to tire Jesus, too. Just think—a very long distance, uphill and downhill, and over rough roads, so that walking was painful and very tiresome for his sacred feet."

"Poor Jesus!" murmured the child lovingly.

"Yes, poor Jesus! And all because he loved us so much. Do you remember how, years before, when the Child Jesus stayed behind in the temple at Jerusalem, and Mary and Joseph were three days looking for him, he told them he must be about his Father's business?"

"I remember, Mommy."

"His whole life was given up to that work for his Father. Jesus came to save the world, and every step he took, every breath he drew, was to help onward that business of his Father. So he made the journey from Galilee to Judea, as part of his labor for the salvation of the world. Great crowds of people pressed about him along the way, some lame, some sick, others blind, and all begging to be cured and made well again, besides wanting to hear the words of Jesus. Upon every side were those he had healed and comforted, and taught the love of God. They, of course, had told their relatives and friends of the wonderful favors Jesus had granted them, so always the crowd grew larger, Carina, and everywhere beside the road more persons were waiting to cry out their misery and trouble to Jesus of Nazareth who was passing through their land.

"It was toward evening of a very hard day that some mothers who had fetched their children with them out into the country where Jesus was, tried to go near the Lord that he might place his hands upon the little ones and give them his blessing. Now the disciples loved their Master, and seeing his face so pale and tired, their devotion to Jesus made them scold the women and tell them to go away."

"But Jesus didn't let them!" said Carina quickly.

"No, dear; he knew the disciples only meant to spare him because he was so weary, but he knew, too, that the mothers loved him, and above all he knew that he himself loved the children dearly. I think, Carina, that Jesus must sympathize very much with the love of mothers for their children, because mothers feel so deeply that only God can really protect the helpless, heedless, little ones, and mothers know from how many dangers children are shielded every day of their lives. We have to put a great deal of trust in God, Carina, and those mothers in the Bible were very anxious indeed to obtain Jesus' blessing for their children, and his care and protection over them. When the disciples told them not to disturb the Master, their hearts grew very heavy. They were terribly disappointed, but they would have gone quietly away, only Jesus would not allow them to leave. The Bible tells us that he rebuked the disciples, which means he made them feel that what they said and did displeased him, and he commanded the mothers to bring the children to him."

"And what did Jesus say, Mommy?"

"He said, 'Let the children come to me, and do not prevent them; for the Kingdom of Heaven belongs to such as these.'"[47]

"Then Jesus meant the children didn't bother him at all, Mommy? He was glad they came to see him and get his blessing?"

"Yes, darling; and he took them into his arms and blessed them. They were very dear to him, and they belonged to his kingdom in heaven. They had never offended the heavenly Father, and were his true

---

[47] Matthew 19:14

children. In that way, those innocent little ones, Carina, were the tiny brothers and sisters of Jesus, Who is God's divine Son."

"Our Father Who art in heaven," said Carina slowly; "and he is the Father of Jesus, too. Then am I Jesus' little sister?" her eyes very big and earnest.

"Yes, sweetheart. Don't ever forget. As long as you are like the children the Savior blessed—humble and good and obedient—you are the little sister of Jesus and belong to his Kingdom of Heaven. Those mothers in the Bible were very grateful and happy when Jesus held their children in his arms, and they went home with hearts full of love for him because he had been so kind to their little ones."

Carina looked very serious.

"Mommy, you love everyone who loves me, don't you?"

"Of course I do."

"And those mothers couldn't help loving Jesus because he loved the children. Mommy, would Jesus ever, ever in all my life, be too busy with big people to listen to Carina?"

"Never. He has a special love for children, dear, and he has told big people that in order to please him they must be like the little children. We have his own words to show us what he thinks about children going to him. Not a holy prophet, nor even an angel, gave us the message, Carina, but Jesus himself. Aren't the words plain?—'Let the children come to me, and do not prevent them.' It is a very beautiful invitation, Carina, for you, and a positive command for us older people, as it was for the disciples. Jesus loved the little ones, and will always love them, and I believe that his blessing is always coming upon them like it did that evening he raised them is his arms and blessed them, in presence of the people. He was worn and tired then, but not too busy to call the mothers back. He can never be tired anymore, because he is glorious in heaven. And his love has not changed."

"I'm glad, Mommy. I hope Jesus is blessing me now. Don't you?"

"Yes, sweetheart. I'm sure he is. And now, good night, little daughter."

Discussion Questions

1. How do you feel after a long, hard day of work, play, and activity? Is it hard not to complain? Is it hard not to be grouchy and impatient? When this happens, how can you imitate Jesus?
2. Have you ever tried to protect someone when they are tired? To save them from more work and stress? How do you show the people you love that you love them?
3. Jesus invites the little children to come to him. How can we go to Jesus? Name several ways that we can be with him. How can seeing him as our brother change the way we pray and the way we relate to him?

✠ Growing In Holiness

Just as in this Gospel story, Jesus wishes to bestow his blessing upon each of us. We can "do Jesus" to those we love by blessing them in his place. Renew the practice of blessing each other (saying, "May God bless you in the name of the Father, and of the Son, and of the Holy Spirit" while tracing the Sign of the Cross with your thumb on the other's forehead) before bedtime and before leaving the house each day. (You may use holy water for this if desired.) St. Dominic believed the Sign of the Cross to be the most powerful of all Christian prayers. The practice of blessing each other—and ourselves—with the Sign of the Cross each day protects us (and those we love) from Satan and his temptations while reminding us of God's providential care for us.

📖 Searching Scripture – Mark 10:13-16

And people were bringing children to him that he might touch them, but the disciples rebuked them. When Jesus saw this he became indignant and said to them, "Let the children come to me; do not prevent them, for the kingdom of God belongs to such as these. Amen, I say to you, whoever does not accept the kingdom of God like a child will not enter it." Then he embraced them and blessed them, placing his hands on them.

✓ **Checking the Catechism**

1. *Which is the chief sacramental used in the Church?* The chief sacramental used in the Church is the Sign of the Cross.

2. *Why do we make the Sign of the Cross?* We make the sign of the cross to show that we are Christians and to profess our belief in the chief mysteries of our religion.

3. *What is holy water?* Holy water is water blessed by the priest with solemn prayer to beg God's blessing on those who use it, and protection from the powers of darkness.

⋆REVIEW⋆ Adult Catechism

No. 351. . . . Among the sacramentals . . . are blessings, which are the praise of God and a prayer to obtain his gifts . . . (See CCC Nos. 1667-1672 and 1677-1678.)

Carina and the Eight Beatitudes

"Mommy," said Carina, her blue eyes very earnest, "what are the Battitous?"

She was more wide awake than usual at bedtime. Grandma had taken her to Vespers at four o'clock, and there had been a sermon. But poor Carina had listened to nearly nothing, for the reason that the opening remark about Beatitudes had set her little head wondering. When Carina began to wonder, she did not leave off soon. All through the service, and all the way home in the wintry dusk, Carina kept reminding herself, "The Battitous—I must ask Mommy."

Now she was alone with her mother at last, and the eager question would be answered.

"The Battitous?" Mommy echoed. Somehow Carina's way of saying the word did not at first make her mother think of anything in the Bible.

"Yes—the Batittous Jesus told the people about," closing her eyes with a sigh of comfort because at last her troubled little head could rest.

"Oh!" said Mommy. "Why, the Beatitudes are what you and I call the *Blesseds*. Don't you remember?"

"Is that it?" astonished. "But I didn't understand, Mommy, and I wish you'd tell me that story tonight. It was such big words in church," she explained, "and when I asked Grandma she said, 'Oh, it's too much for you to understand, dear.' Wait till I tell her those Battitous are our *Blesseds,* Mommy, and I heard about them awfully long ago." Being six years old, Carina considered she had lived a great while.

If you remember how very long it is from one birthday or Christmas to the next one, you will know why Carina felt so terribly old. It often does seem hard to have so many other days—just plain days—before Christmas or the Fourth of July or a birthday, and yet I suppose we need plain days so we can rest.

"The Beatitudes," began Mommy, "are told us in the Sermon on the Mount. Who preached that sermon, Carina?"

"Jesus, Mommy. Because he saw such a big crowd of people waiting to be taught; and he went up into a mountain, high, so that they could see him, and he told them about the *Blesseds.*"

"Fine, Carina! He understood how much they needed those lessons about who are really blessed, because he knew every secret of their hearts. Those people had worldly ideas instead of heavenly ones, and craved for exactly the opposites of all the things the Savior longed for them to possess. Think how they must have stared, Carina, at the new strange things Jesus of Nazareth was telling them! If they were stirring and restless in the beginning, looking up at the figure upon the mountain, the first words

Jesus spoke must have surprised them into perfect quiet. Listen, Carina: Through the stillness comes that tender voice of Jesus, in a new message to the old world: 'Blessed are the poor in spirit, for theirs is the Kingdom of Heaven.'"[48]

"They couldn't have liked it, Mommy. They liked to be rich, and—and grand, and covered with jewelry, and better than anybody else. And full of airs," Carina finished, for that expressed everything.

"Quite so. You see, they weren't bothering about that Kingdom of Heaven Jesus was promising them, if they kept loving the wealth of this world. They were living for what they could find here. And perhaps Carina, some defiance shown in their faces, or at least arose in their hearts, because the next Beatitude was one of warning against pride and anger:[49] 'Blessed are the meek, for they will inherit the land.'[50] Meekness was despised before Jesus came. Even the Jews sought revenge for every wrong. You know, dear, they claimed, 'eye for eye, tooth for tooth.'"[51]

"They wanted," said Carina wisely, "to get even with people."

"I'm afraid they did. They couldn't imagine the meekness that suffers everything in silence. But you see, Carina, they hadn't either heard or thought of that wonderful lesson our Lord told us—'. . . learn from me, for I am meek and humble of heart.'[52] So

---

[48] Matthew 5:3

[49] This is the order according to the Douay Rheims translation.

[50] Matthew 5:5

[51] Exodus 21:24

[52] Matthew 11:29

the second Beatitude was as much a shock to their proud, haughty minds as the first. They must have listened even more anxiously as Jesus went on: 'Blessed are they who mourn, for they will be comforted.'[53] Now everybody likes fun and pleasure, but who likes to mourn?"

"I think nobody, Mommy. It's nicer to laugh." Carina would be honest at any cost.

"Of course it is nicer, and ever so much more pleasant. But Jesus on the Mount plainly declared that people who are in grief and trouble, those who can't find it in their hearts to laugh, are blessed. And he added those sweet words, 'for they shall be comforted.'"

"Comforted by Jesus," said Carina softly. "He must comfort them, because he says so."

"Surely. And as that listening mass of people grows more and more astonished, Jesus says: 'Blessed are they who hunger and thirst for righteousness, for they will be satisfied.'[54] Imagine worldly people who love good things to eat and drink, being told about those who hunger and thirst simply after pure goodness! I think by that time those surprised multitudes had entirely lost their first feeling of rebellion at the strange lessons they were being taught. They could only listen meekly, Carina, already coming in the way of that promise that the meek should possess the land."

"The real land, Mommy?"

---

[53] Matthew 5:4
[54] Matthew 5:6

"Sometimes, dear, even the real land, in the sense that those who keep their tempers and are patient, can usually see clearly in matters of worldly interest; when we grow excited and unreasonable, we're not only doing wrong, but we are putting ourselves at a disadvantage with the calm, sensible people."

"I see," said Carina, sighing. "One day I was cross with Amy Deans—I was in a dreadful temper—and I snatched her doll away from her. It broke, Mommy —do you remember?—and I had to give her my other one. The nice one with the brown eyes and the curls?"

"I do remember."

"Well, if I'd thought of that *Blessed,* Mommy, and kept meek, Amy wouldn't have my best doll." Carina's small mouth set firmly. She was making up her mind not to lose either dolls or temper in the future. She really did miss that brown-eyed doll very much. And here was a *Blessed,* a little piece of that wonderful Sermon on the Mount that Jesus himself preached, which exactly fit into Carina's case. She decided not to forget it.

"And when," her mother went on, "we don't gain any earthly possession by being meek, we still gain the promise of the beautiful land we call heaven. Don't you know, 'The Beautiful Land on High'?"

"Oh yes, Mommy. I know the song."

"Well, while perhaps those people were beginning to have some idea of the happiness of heaven, Jesus reminded them they were sinners: 'Blessed are the merciful, for they will be shown mercy.'[55] We each

---

[55] Matthew 5:7

and all need the mercy of God."

"I know what that means," sighed Carina; "it means not to get cross with Daisy if she gets cross with me, 'cause I do 'most everything wrong, and I don't want God to be cross with me."

"Exactly. We can all find some chance to show mercy, little one. And possibly showing mercy is the surest way of becoming clean of heart. So the next Beatitude is 'Blessed are the clean of heart, for they will see God.'[56] What a promise that is, Carina!"

"To see him like I see you?" asked Carina. "Just as plainly?"

"Even much more plainly. To see him face to face, and to understand everything we can't understand now; to live in the light and love and peace of our Father in heaven. All this, Carina, for those who are clean of heart."

"Oh Mommy!" Carina breathed. "Am I clean of heart?"

Mommy hugged her closely. "Surely, darling, and you must always stay so. Don't forget what our Lord is bound to give you, for keeping clean of heart. He has promised, and God can't break his word. You shall see God."

"I'll try, Mommy," said Carina, a bit sleepily. "I'd love to see God."

"Two more *Blesseds,* dear. 'Blessed are the peacemakers, for they will be called the children of God.'[57] The Jews were frightened, Carina. Here was another

---

[56] Matthew 5:8
[57] Matthew 5:9

blow at their old way of doing things. They were forever at war, not only with other tribes, but among
themselves, too. And they had always considered
themselves the children of God. Now Jesus of Nazareth, whom we sometimes call by his sweet name
of the 'Prince of Peace,'[58] was teaching them how to
be his brothers, and therefore really and indeed the
children of his heavenly Father. They were to follow
peace, to take peace to others, to make peace where
there had been quarrels and war."

"Like, Mommy, when we quarrel with friends. I
think I won't quarrel with Amy Deans ever anymore."
Unhappy memories flushed Carina's cheeks.

"Then," said Mommy, a little mischief in her smile,
"you will surely be blessed, my darling. And the last
Beatitude—for you're nearly asleep, Carina—is 'Blessed are they who are persecuted for the sake of righteousness, for theirs is the Kingdom of Heaven.'"[59]

'That means the martyrs," said Carina, very, very
sleepily. "And some day—you'll tell me—that story."
She did not hear her mother's "Good night!"

Discussion Questions

1. Make a list of worldly ideas and their opposite
   heavenly ideas. How do your ideas (and your
   family's) fit into this chart? What does Jesus, in
   the teaching of the beatitudes, ask you to change?

[58] Isaiah 9:5
[59] Matthew 5:10

2. How could acquiring the virtue of meekness (controlling your temper, not being too quick to defend yourself, not looking for revenge) make you more like Jesus?
3. "They were living for what they could find here" (page 105). In many ways, people of our American culture are also guilty of this accusation. If you were truly living for your heavenly reward and unconcerned about the wealth and pleasures of this world, what would you need to give up (or change) in your daily habits?

✚ Growing In Holiness

"We can all find some chance to show mercy" (page 108). Cultivate a spirit of mercy, an attitude of forgiveness, a non-judgmental heart. The Our Father assures us that we will be forgiven and shown mercy only as we forgive others. Make this a point of your nightly examination of conscience.

📖 Searching Scripture – Matthew 5:1-10

When he saw the crowds, he went up the mountain, and after he had sat down, his disciples came to him. He began to teach them, saying:

"Blessed are the poor in spirit,
    for theirs is the Kingdom of Heaven.
Blessed are they who mourn,
    for they will be comforted.
Blessed are the meek,

for they will inherit the land.
Blessed are they who hunger and thirst for
    righteousness,
    for they will be satisfied.
Blessed are the merciful,
    for they will be shown mercy.
Blessed are the clean of heart,
    for they will see God.
Blessed are the peacemakers,
    for they will be called children of God.
Blessed are they who are persecuted for the sake
    of righteousness,
    for theirs is the Kingdom of Heaven."

✓ Checking the Catechism

1. *What are the Beatitudes and why are they so called?*
The Beatitudes are a portion of our Lord's Sermon
on the Mount, and they are so called because each
of them holds out a promised reward to those who
practice the virtues they recommend.

2. *What is the meaning and use of the Beatitudes in
general?* A) In general, the Beatitudes embrace
whatever pertains to the perfection of Christian
life, and they invite us to the practice of the highest Christian virtues. B) In different forms they
all promise the same reward, namely, sanctifying
grace in this life and eternal glory in the next. C)
They offer us encouragement and consolation for
every trial and affliction.

★REVIEW★ Adult Catechism

No. 360. The beatitudes are at the heart of Jesus' preaching . . . they depict the very countenance of Jesus and they characterize authentic Christian life. (See CCC Nos. 1716-1717 and 1725-1726.)

Carina and the Miracles

Carina had something of importance upon her mind; it was quite private, so she glanced carefully around to make sure she and Mommy were alone before she whispered:

"Amy's grandfather went to church this morning for the first time in ten years; and Amy's mother told me it was a wonder and a miracle! Mommy, was it?"

"It was a wonder, sweetheart, but no miracle. I'm glad he went." Mommy stroked the frown out of Carina's forehead.

"So'm I," said Carina happily. "I know God was glad to see him there. Seems to me lots of people forget to go. Perhaps because they're so busy. But, Mommy, what's a miracle?"

"What do you think it is?"

"I thought it was just a wonder. And it can't be only a wonder because you said Amy's grandfather was a wonder but no miracle." Carina's forehead was again creased with trouble.

Her mother laughed merrily. "He is, as far as I know, neither a wonder nor a miracle—" Carina

113

looked so hurt that Mommy stopped teasing. "Never mind, dear, I know what you meant."

"A miracle," said Carina thoughtfully, "is, I suppose, something we couldn't do by ourselves."

"That's very good for a start. Miracles are such great wonders, dear, that we can never understand them except as a part of a truth I love to think about. It's in our catechism, Carina, and it's the greatest comfort in the world all through life: *God can do all things and nothing is hard or impossible for him.* Never forget that God can do anything. There is no limit of any sort to his power. And only God's power can work a miracle. The Son of God worked many miracles while he was upon earth, and I shall tell you about a few of them tonight. The servants and followers of our Lord, too, by his divine power, have performed miracles. Now let's understand what a miracle is.

"Could you lift that table, Carina?" pointing to one covered with Carina's picture books.

"Oh no, Mommy! Of course not."

"But suppose ten little girls tried altogether and lifted it—do you think they would be working a miracle?"

"No, Mommy. Because ten little girls could lift almost anything."

"Then, although Carina couldn't lift the table by herself, it could be lifted very easily and naturally, if enough people worked together. Lots of things look impossible at first, and sometimes we cry out, 'We can't,' when what our Father in heaven wishes us to

114

do, Carina, is simply to use the common sense he has given us and try every means within reason. We could move tables and lots of other things if we were not so easily discouraged. Now tell me, Carina: You had scarlet fever, and you recovered. Was your cure a miracle?"

Carina considered. She had been terribly sick, and her head and throat had hurt so that sometimes she cried. But Dr. Walker had given her all sorts of things that make people well, and Mommy and a nurse had between them cared for her day and night. Still, Carina was not sure; it did hurt so, to have scarlet fever, maybe it took a miracle to be cured.

"I was awfully sick," she said doubtfully.

"But every natural means we knew about was used to cure my little girl, and God willed that the doctor should be successful. That you recovered was no miracle, although it was such a big blessing." Mommy's arms clasped Carina tightly.

Carina lay very still. She was happy that Daddy and Mommy were so glad to have her with them.

"Grandma says," said Carina after a while, "people pray for money and expect it to drop from heaven. She says they ought to work for the money, instead of being lazy and asking for miracles to happen."

"Grandma's ideas are good, Carina, even if not beautiful. For money to fall from heaven would be a real miracle. You see, now, don't you, that a mere wonder is not a miracle?"

"Yes, Mommy."

"This great universe, this big world, dear, and all

115

the creatures in it, are ruled by laws made by God himself. There are laws for the sun and the moon and all the stars. There are laws for the rivers and the oceans."

"And laws for us, Mommy?"questioned Carina.

"Yes. You are a tiny girl, and Mommy is a grown woman. By some of those great laws by which God rules all that he has made, we were created and we have grown. The flowers come in their regular turns, the fruits grow ripe, the leaves die; spring returns, and the old law begins over again. You see, Carina, there is a great order in all God does; he created everything that is, and he made rules to govern every single creature."

"Just as we have rules to run the house," said Carina.

"Something like that," smiled Mommy. "Well, Carina, if God works a wonder that means he puts aside in that instance the rules that govern his creation— or what you will often hear grownup people call 'the laws of nature'—then he performs a miracle."

"I don't understand, Mommy." Carina never let her mother go on until she was satisfied.

"If water running in a brook comes to the top of a hill, Carina, what does it do?" Mommy spoke very slowly.

"The top of a hill? Why, it tumbles down, of course."

"You never saw water climb up a hill, did you?"

"No, Mommy," laughing.

"A law of nature forces water to run down a hill. Another law makes your geraniums and pansies turn their faces to the sun, not away from it. Still another law causes us to be born tiny, weak infants and gradually grow up into strong men and women. If the brook when it reached the top of the hill, did not rush down, that would mean that the natural order was set aside, and that God had worked a miracle. He would interfere with his own laws."

"But then," said Carina, "does God ever do that?"

"He did, and he does work miracles. Don't forget that answer in the catechism: *God can do all things and nothing is hard or impossible for him.* He made the world out of nothing; and surely he controls what he has made."

"Out of nothing!" Carina repeated. "And it is so big!"

"It certainly is; and yet, little girl, the God who made the great, wide world made every wee flower in it. Think of those forget-me-nots you picked for me today. Each tiny, blue flower God made; they grew this year in the place where they grew last year and where they will grow next year, by one of his laws that is being obeyed all over creation. The first forget-me-not he knew, and he will know the last. And in his laws that forget-me-not has a place, as surely as the mighty ocean. The flower needs earth, water, and light, or it cannot grow. If suddenly out of that vase on the mantel, forget-me-nots should grow, they would exist by a miracle because the earth, water, and light are by God's laws necessary for the life of a plant."

"I understand, now, Mommy, what a miracle is."

"Then let me tell you a little bit, darling, about some of the miracles of Jesus. There is one he worked directly after he came down from the Sermon on the Mount. It was upon a poor man from whom everybody ran away, and who was, humanly speaking, without any hope of ever living among people again, because he was a leper. That meant he had a dreadful disease which nobody could cure. Leprosy was so terrible that anyone who had it had to stay outside of the city. Now this poor leper who had no friends and no home, and whose disease would soon kill him, believed Jesus to be the Son of God. He knelt down close to our Lord and with his whole heart and soul he cried out: 'Lord, if you wish, you can make me clean!'[60] The Bible tells us that great multitudes were following Jesus, and we know many of these people went after him simply out of curiosity—not all of them had faith. The poor leper paid no attention to anyone but Jesus. That sick man, an outcast from the world, knew that God was before him and that God, as the catechism says, can do anything. So he knelt down and uttered his prayer in the faces of those who did not believe, as well as in the presence of Jesus' true friends. 'If you wish,' he cried. The God who created him, the God who holds heaven and earth in his hand, need only will that the horrid leprosy would be healed. And what happened, Carina?"

"The leper got well?" Carina asked eagerly.

"Jesus stretched forth his hand and touched the suffering man. Our Lord spoke, too, saying, 'I do will

---

[60] Matthew 8:2

it. Be made clean.'[61] And instantly that poor leper was well and strong. Jesus told the man, too, to go to the priest and offer the gift Moses had commanded.

"Oh, Carina, if only we could always remember to show our gratitude when God does a favor for us! It's so easy to ask, dear, and so natural when we are miserable or suffering or even uncomfortable! But lots of times we forget to say 'Thank you!' as even the weakest kind of politeness would do. It's a plain lesson to us, when Jesus reminds the healed leper to make his thanksgiving."

"Did the leper do it, Mommy?"

"I think so. I don't want to think he didn't. It seems to me that a man as earnest as he was would not forget to be grateful. Now, Carina, I shall tell you about one more miracle tonight. Do you remember the centurion who came to Jesus?"

"No, Mommy. And I don't know what a centurion is."

"A centurion was something like a captain in our army. He had a hundred Roman soldiers under his orders, making up what we would call a company. The centurion met Jesus when he had entered Capernaum. The man was very much worried and excited, and we are told he came 'appealing.' He quickly told what was troubling him: 'Lord, my servant is lying at home paralyzed, suffering dreadfully.'[62] To be paralyzed, Carina, is another condition which no earthly means can cure. Then Jesus said to the centurion, 'I will

---

[61] Matthew 8:3
[62] Matthew 8:6

come and cure him.'[63] But the humility and the faith of that man were both very great. Listen to his answer: 'Lord, I am not worthy to have you enter under my roof; only say the word and my servant will be healed.'[64] He knew that time and place make no difference to God. He knew that our Lord need only will the cure of the servant. Besides, he felt that he was not deserving of a personal visit from Jesus, that his house was not worthy of such a guest.

"I never can be sure which was more beautiful, Carina, that centurion's mighty faith or his wonderful humility. He was not even of the Jewish people, who had been taught to look for the coming of the Savior. We are positive he was of the Gentiles, as the Jews called those who were not of their own faith, because Jesus marveled at the centurion's words and told his followers that he had not found such great faith in Israel. Turning afterward to the waiting centurion, Jesus rewarded that immense faith with which the man had prayed to him. 'You may go,' said Jesus, 'as you have believed, let it be done for you.'[65] You see there was no doubt in the prayer, no wonder whether God would grant it or not; and there was no delay in the cure of the servant."

"He got well that minute, Mommy?"

"Yes. Far away from where the centurion begged the favor of Jesus, in an instant the servant was healed. Imagine his astonishment, Carina, when he

---

[63] Matthew 8:7
[64] Matthew 8:8
[65] Matthew 8:13

suddenly found himself free from his annoying sickness! It's such a comfort to know that we may pray for others as well as ourselves. Jesus hears all our prayers, and he answers them, every one, although not always in the way we wished. No prayer is ever wasted, Carina. We may forget most of the prayers we say during the years we live. But God never will."

"Mommy," said Carina very softly, "I think that when I was sick you must have prayed as hard as the centurion."

"Perhaps," said her mother quite as softly, "perhaps I did."

Discussion Questions

1. Talk about some of the wonders of God's creation. What are some of God's wonders that you have experienced? Take a moment to thank God out loud for these wonders.

2. "If only we could always remember to show our gratitude when God does a favor for us!" (page 119) When is the last time you thanked God for something? When is the last time you have thanked your parents, or your friends, or your brother or sister, or your teacher? Express your thanks at least three times today. Work on having a grateful heart and offering thanks to others often.

3. "It's such a comfort to know that we may pray for others as well as ourselves" (page 121). For whom

or what can you—should you—pray? Do you believe that God answers your prayers? Do you believe that God can do all things—that nothing is impossible for him? Share a time when a prayer was answered in an unexpected way.

✝ Growing In Holiness

When you are worried or anxious, pray this simple prayer: "God, I believe you can do all things." Then trust that God will answer your prayer in the very best possible way for you. His answer may not be what you expect or when you expect. But trust that his answer will be according to what is best for you. Remember to thank God—as Venerable Solanus Casey would recommend—"ahead of time" for answering your prayers.

📖 Searching Scripture – Matthew 8:1-13

When Jesus came down from the mountain, great crowds followed him. And then a leper approached, did him homage, and said, "Lord, if you wish, you can make me clean." He stretched out his hand, touched him, and said, "I will do it. Be made clean." His leprosy was cleansed immediately. Then Jesus said to him, "See that you tell no one, but go show yourself to the priest, and offer the gift that Moses prescribed; that will be proof for them."

When he entered Capernaum, a centurion approached him and appealed to him, saying, "Lord, my servant is lying at home paralyzed, suffering dreadfully." He said to him, "I will come and cure him." The centurion said in reply, "Lord, I am not worthy to have you enter under my roof; only say the word and my servant will be healed. For I too am a person subject to authority, with soldiers subject to me. And I say to one, 'Go,' and he goes; and to another, 'Come here,' and he comes; and to my slave, 'Do this,' and he does it." When Jesus heard this, he was amazed and said to those following him, "Amen, I say to you, in no one in Israel have I found such faith. I say to you, many will come from the east and the west, and will recline with Abraham, Isaac, and Jacob at the banquet in the Kingdom of Heaven, but the children of the kingdom will be driven out into the outer darkness, where there will be wailing and grinding of teeth." And Jesus said to the centurion, "You may go; as you have believed, let it be done for you." And at that very hour [his] servant was healed.

✓ **Checking the Catechism**

1. *Can God do all things?* God can do all things, and nothing is hard or impossible to him.
2. *When is a thing said to be "impossible"?* A thing is said to be "impossible" when it cannot be done. Many things that are impossible for creatures are possible for God.
3. *What is prayer?* Prayer is the lifting up of our minds and hearts to God, to adore him, to thank him for his benefits, to ask his forgiveness, and to beg of him all the graces we need whether for soul or body.

4. *What assurance have we that God always hears and rewards our prayers, though he may not grant what we ask?* We have the assurance of our Lord himself that God always hears and rewards our prayers, though he may not grant what we ask; for Christ said: "Ask and it shall be given you," and "if you ask the Father anything in my name, he will give it to you."

⭐REVIEW⭐ Adult Catechism

No. 534. [The prayer of] intercession consists in asking on behalf of another. It conforms us and unites us to the prayer of Jesus who intercedes with the Father for all, especially sinners. (See CCC Nos. 2634-2636 and 2647.)

Carina and the Parables

When children are as little as Carina, of course, they hear and see ever so many things every single day that they cannot understand. Daddy or Mommy, or somebody, says or does something that is new. And children, who are always learning or trying to learn, want what was said or done explained to them. That's why big people often call little folks "curious." Certainly, they are as curious as any kitty cat that ever was, and they can ask questions from breakfast time till bedtime without stopping. They ought to be curious; if they weren't, how would they stop being tiny babies who don't know anything? It is too bad when a little boy or girl is afraid to ask questions. That little boy or girl keeps on wondering, and if he or she grows tired of wondering, the next thing is to start guessing. And, oh dear, sometimes that guessing is all wrong!

Carina didn't mind asking questions; she knew her mother would answer them—even silly ones. Often the questions didn't seem silly till after Mommy answered, but anyway it was a good thing to learn how silly one could be. Mommy never told anybody else, and it was such a comfort to Carina to know that all those talks in the dim bedroom were only for Mommy and herself—and their guardian angels, as Mommy sometimes said.

Now Carina had heard about parables when the Gospel was read in church. And she was positive parables were different from miracles, but that was about all.

"Mommy," said she, "isn't everything in the Bible true?"

"Certainly, Carina. The Holy Spirit caused every word to be written. He is God, and God is Truth."

"I thought so. Then, how can parables not be true?"

"How do you mean, dear?"

"Well!" Carina was quite embarrassed. "You see," and the little girl lowered her voice, "Amy told me they were stories."

Mommy smothered a laugh in Carina's curls because she did not want to hurt Carina's feelings.

"Stories, in a way, but a better word would be 'lessons.' There is a long word which exactly explains what a parable is. It may be too long for you, Carina."

"What is it, Mommy?" Carina eagerly asked. "I know lots of big words—really I do."

"A parable is a similitude," said Mommy slowly.

"Oh!" Carina stared. That truly was a hard one.

"And, let me see, a similitude you might call a likening of one thing to something else. For instance, if I wanted to show you what a mother's love is for her little son or daughter, I might tell you a story

about a bird and her little ones—how the mother
bird works to feed the babies, how she keeps them
warm under her wings, how she will even try to protect them when a cruel bird like a hawk, or else a
pussy cat, wants to kill them. Now if I told you all
about a family of robins or bluebirds to make you
see how very strong a mother's love is, and if I meant
the story to teach you how a human mother loves
her little children, that story would be a similitude.
Do you understand any better, dear?"

"Yes, Mommy. Only, our Lord's Apostles were big
men like Daddy, and Jesus told them parables. Could-
n't he tell them everything the way it was, and not
in stories?"

"He could have, Carina. But he took a simple, more
loving way. With God, we are all children."

"Even the president, Mommy?" Carina's eyes were
wide with wonder.

"Even the president. If we learned all Jesus had
to teach, it would be much harder for us to remember by plain, severe orders. Instead, Jesus took the
simple, everyday matters of our lives and used them
to explain to us the ways of God. When he called Peter and James and John from the fishing nets, he
told them they would after that be fishers of men.
They knew what fishing meant: Patient waiting and
hard pulling. They knew there were storms at sea,
and dark windy nights, and sometimes fishermen
were drowned at their work. Jesus called them to
save men. They would need patience and strength,
there would be troubles and pain and terrors to face.

Many of them would die at their work—they would be martyred for the Faith they preached to the world. Could anything have been truer, Carina, than the similitude Jesus gave them?"

"No, Mommy." Carina liked the idea that the fishers of the sea should be made fishers of men. She had heard people talking about "labors for souls." Carina knew labor meant hard work, and the way Mommy explained the lives of St. Peter and St. Paul and St. John, they worked very much harder saving souls from sin and misery than they had worked catching fish in the sea.

"Another day, dear, Jesus sat eating with sinners. The Pharisees—those proud Jews who gloried in themselves and looked down upon the rest of the world—went at once to question the disciples. The Pharisees pretended to be horrified at the sight of Jesus associating with the unfortunate publicans and common sinners, and asked why he did so. Before the disciples could answer, Jesus himself instructed those miserable Jews. Do you know what he said?"

"No, Mommy."

"'Those who are well do not need a physician, but the sick do.'[66] Wasn't that a beautiful way to show them why he came upon earth? They all knew who a physician was: He was one to cure them, to take away their pain, to quiet their fears. People who are well don't need a doctor. They never send for one. His work is not for the healthy and strong. So Jesus explained that he was like a physician. He came to cure,

---

[66] Matthew 9:12

to comfort, to make strong—not our bodies, but our souls. The human doctor works for our bodies, which must someday die; Jesus works for our souls, which not only won't, but never can, die. Often, he cures both body and soul, but he never refuses to cure the soul—that soul which bears his own image. He comes to us in our troubles and selfishness, and all our naughtiness, Carina, and shows us how to be cured. He is not horrified, as the Pharisees thought he was, but he longs to make us well, because he died in order that we might live in heaven with him, and the sick in soul—they are the willful sinners—cannot enter heaven."

"Will he cure every sinner, Mommy?"

"Every single one who will accept him as the Physician. All the sins in the world may be wiped out at the Foot of the Cross upon which Jesus died. There is no limit whatever to the mercy of God, and no soul, no matter how black and ugly with sin, that the Precious Blood will not make white and beautiful like that soul was upon the day of its Baptism. But the parables, Carina—we are talking away and not getting ahead with our story."

"I'm not sleepy yet, Mommy," said Carina earnestly.

"Then let us have the parable about the sower, or the farmer, who went out to sow his seed. There were a great many seeds, Carina, and every seed might have succeeded in growing, but a great many did not, and we are told why: The sower scattered the seed right and left, generously and faithfully, and for his part of the work the harvest should have been a huge one. But everything did not depend simply upon the sower. You can understand that the kind of ground which received the seed would make a difference, for one thing. And there were other obstacles, too, which prevented the sower gathering a big crop from his field. Some of the seed he scattered fell by the wayside, and at once the hungry little birds flew down and ate that seed up. That was the first lot of seed that went to waste; in that part of the field there would be a bare spot at harvest time, although the seed itself had been perfectly good. Then there were places in the ground where the earth was only a very thin layer, and underneath was stone. The stone was cold and lifeless and could not feed the roots which sprang from the seed. So the plant grew rapidly upwards towards the sun, making at first a very promising sight for the farmer. But there were no roots to speak of, because the stone would not feed any, and by and by the sun became terribly hot for the poor plant standing so high with no strength to support it. If it had been a healthy sort, the sun would have cheered it up and helped it grow. Instead it grew weaker and weaker in the heat and light and at last it withered away simply for the want of roots."

"Poor plant!" said Carina, who hated to see anything fade.

"There was still another portion of seed which never brought forth any fruit: it fell where thorns had made their home, and when the seed grew up the thorns appeared with it. The worst of it was that the thorns grew much faster than the sower's seed. They pushed ahead—strong and ugly and greedy—and soon they had completely killed the struggling seed which the sower had scattered. Jesus says the thorns 'choked' the seed. It had no chance with the evil growth it met."

"But some seed grew, Mommy?" Carina anxiously asked.

"Yes. In the parable, some seed fell upon good ground—no stones, no thorns to torment it. That seed brought forth fruit in great abundance. Some of it yielded one hundred times more than it had been itself, some sixty times, some thirty. It seems as if the successful seed made up to the sower for all that was lost.

"Now this is a parable, Carina, and later, Jesus explained it to his disciples. The sower is God, and the seed is his Word. All kinds of people hear that Word of God, but not all heed it. Some listen carelessly, make no effort to understand, and at the first temptation, let Satan steal God's message out of their hearts. Jesus calls these people the ones who received the seed by the wayside. They were robbed of it at once. If they had kept in safe places and not gone roaming where temptations were around like thieves upon an unprotected wayside, they might have kept the Word of God in their hearts."

"And the seed that had no roots, Mommy, because there were stones? Did Jesus explain about that?"

"Yes, indeed. There are plenty of people, shallow people we call them, who have no depth in anything.

They are a little of everything, carried away by anything new, whether it is good or bad, and such people are never to be relied upon."

"The kind that spend their money on anything? And never do what they've promised to do?" Carina questioned. She had a wee bit of fear she herself was not so very much to be relied upon.

"Sometimes such people do spend money foolishly," said Mommy, but she kissed Carina comfortingly. "And yet there are plenty who never buy foolishly, but who are not to be depended upon in other ways. Don't you know the way some people—even little people like you—are quick to offer to do this or that, just aching to be obliging, and so on, but their zeal wears off in about two minutes, and when the time comes for their promises to be kept, they are apt to have forgotten them entirely? Those are more like the people who will hear God's Word with joy, rush to obey it, and suddenly, when any trial or difficulty rises up before them, simply turn about and run as fast away from it as they first imagined they'd run to meet it. They have no depth, no roots, and like the grain that grew up above the stones withered away in the sun, such people wither away in the dryness of duty.

"Then the thorns, Carina—Jesus compares them with the cares of this world and its riches. Suppose someone received the Word of God and in spite of having received it spent all his time and thoughts upon the things of this world; always worrying over money and clothes and getting ahead in their job—"

"And children," sighed Carina.

"No," Mommy laughed, "children are bright spots. We'll only consider dark spots. Above all, suppose a man is fairly sick about how wealthy he can become, selfish with everybody, jealous of others who succeed, willing to be mean and dishonest if only he can get ahead of the rest. Don't you see that these cares, like the hideous thorns, will choke the Word of God to death in that man's heart? Why, there simply won't be room for anything except the horrid thorns. His soul will be one of those sad places in God's kingdom where no fruit is found."

"It's very discouraging," sighed Carina.

"It would be, if it weren't for the part of the seed that fell upon good ground. That means that when people receive the Word of God with faith, when they understand it and hold fast to it, that they glorify the Sower, who is God, by bringing forth fruit abundantly. The fruit means good works: Kindness to others, love for our Father in heaven, patience and gratitude in our little lives. We need the patience for our troubles and hurts—our disappointments and toothaches, Carina—and the gratitude for all that is good and pleasant about us."

"For Daddy and Mommy," Carina said, "and— flowers and—parties and—Christmas and—" she paused, thinking of what should come next.

"Yes, Christmas above all, dear," said Mommy, "when Jesus came to live for us, and teach us by parables, and at last to buy heaven for us by dying upon the Cross."

Discussion Questions

1. Are you curious and full of wonder? Name three things about God that you are curious about. How can you find the answers? Are there answers to your questions or are they part of the Mystery that is God?

2. Why did Jesus teach in parables? What is a parable? Why is it easier to learn from a "story"?

3. Discuss the four places the seed was sown. Think of times in your life when you demonstrated each of these four places—times when we make no effort to follow Jesus and give in at the first temptation, times when you have been shallow and unreliable, times when you have only cared about the things of this world, and times when you have truly imitated Jesus by being kind and loving.

Growing In Holiness

We have all had times when our faith has not borne fruit, when we have become lax in our faith and swayed by every temptation that comes our way. Take time right now to review your life, your habits, the way you spend your time, how you relate to people. What needs to change in order to become more like the fruitful seed—to become closer to the person Jesus calls us to be? Try to examaine your conscience more often (preferrably at least daily). Begin to receive the Sacraments of Reconcilation and Holy Eucharist more often too in order to strengthen your will to become more Christ-like and to produce more fruit for the Kingdom of God.

📖 **Searching Scripture – Matthew 13:1-14 and Matthew 13:18-23**

On that day, Jesus went out of the house and sat down by the sea. Such large crowds gathered around him that he got into a boat and sat down, and the whole crowd stood along the shore. And he spoke to them at length in parables, saying: "A sower went out to sow. And as he sowed, some seed fell on the path, and birds came and ate it up. Some fell on rocky ground, where it had little soil. It sprang up at once because the soil was not deep, and when the sun rose it was scorched, and it withered for lack of roots. Some seed fell among thorns, and the thorns grew up and choked it. But some seed fell on rich soil, and produced fruit, a hundred or sixty or thirty-old. Whoever has ears ought to hear."

The disciples approached him and said, "Why do you speak to them in parables?" He said to them in reply, "Because knowledge of the mysteries of the Kingdom of Heaven has been granted to you, but to them it has not been granted. To anyone who has, more will be given and he will grow rich; from anyone who has not, even what he has will be taken away. This is why I speak to them in parables, because 'they look but do not see and hear but do not listen or understand.'"

———

"Hear then the parable of the sower. The seed sown on the path is the one who hears the word of the kingdom without understanding it, and the evil one comes and steals away what was sown in his heart. The seed sown on rocky ground is the one who hears the word and receives it at once with joy. But he has no root and lasts only for a time. When some tribulation or persecution comes because of the word, he immediately falls away. The seed sown among thorns is the one who hears the word, but then worldly anxiety and the lure of riches choke the word and it bears no fruit. But the seed sown on rich soil is the one who hears the word and understands it, who indeed bears fruit and yields a hundred or sixty or thirtyfold."

(You may also wish to read Matthew 9:10-13, which contains Jesus' comment on who has need of a physician.)

✓ Checking the Catechism

1. *Why did God make you?* God made me to know Him, to love Him, and to serve Him in this world, and to be happy with Him forever in the next.
2. *What is the Holy Scripture or Bible?* The Holy Scripture or Bible is the collection of sacred, inspired writings through which God has made known to us many revealed truths.

REVIEW Adult Catechism

No. 382. Fortitude assures firmness in difficulties and constancy in the pursuit of the good. (See CCC Nos. 1808 and 1837.)

The Pharisee and the Tax Collector

The sun shone brightly into Carina's playroom, the canary was singing in his cage; but things were not happy. Toys and dolls lay upon the floor, mingled with the wreck of Carina's blue and white china clock.

Three excited little girls were close to crying, and one was very angry indeed. Daisy Montrose, good-natured and lovable generally, had stamped her little foot and clenched her dimpled hands. Amy Deans was loud and scornful, and Carina had said, "I think you're horrid, and I wish you'd go home, Amy Deans!"

"I never pushed her," Amy returned, her eyes flashing. "Daisy fell over and hit the old clock herself!"

"I didn't!" cried Daisy, stamping her foot for the second time. "I don't tell stories, Amy Deans, and you do! I wouldn't be you—"

"Pharisee!" said Amy haughtily, "That's what you are! Pharisee!"

Amy was two years older than Daisy and Carina. For that reason, she usually led in whatever they did. Amy loved big words, although she often used them without knowing what they really meant, and she had a very unladylike habit of calling names when she was angry. She was sure "Pharisee" sounded very big and high-flown, and she happened to know at least part of its meaning.

"No," said Carina in a quick burst of temper, "you are a Pharisee yourself, Amy Deans! You always want to win, and to be first, and you did hit Daisy with your doll 'cause I saw you, and Daisy doesn't tell stories, and—and I don't know whether you do or not—"

At that moment, Mommy walked into the playroom.

The canary had stopped singing, and suddenly the room was very still. Amy fidgeted with the buckle of her belt, Daisy stood with dropped eyelids, Carina stared questioningly into Mommy's face. What would Mommy think of losing one's temper and being rude to a friend? Carina's bright red cheeks grew brighter still.

"Well?" said Mommy cheerfully. "There has been an accident." Mommy's glance had at once taken in the broken clock upon the floor. "Is anyone hurt?"

Carina flew to her mother at that, and hid a few tears against Mommy's arm.

"No one is hurt; thank you, Mommy," Carina sobbed. "It's my clock—it fell and—and—"

"I suppose it was my fault," said Amy, making a great effort.

"No," Daisy eagerly put in, "I hit it somehow as Amy and I were both reaching for the doll."

"Then let's pick up the pieces," said Mommy, "and

be glad nobody was struck as it fell."

"Tweet, tweet!" chirped the canary, as though he fully approved.

But nobody felt very lively even after the pieces were picked up and Carina's mother had placed something in the bare spot upon the shelf. Amy and Daisy soon went home, and Carina was very lonesome because Grandma was out and Mommy had friends visiting.

"I wish," Carina sighed to herself, "I hadn't called Amy a Pharisee! But no matter how long I keep wishing, I can't get the word back. Isn't it awful?" Carina stood by the window looking out. "Last night I stood here," her busy little brain went on, "and the houses were just like now, and the streetlights were lighted and the mailman whistled the same way. But I hadn't called Amy a Pharisee. So it was different. I wish the company would go! And I wish supper was over!"

Sigh after sigh was breathed against the cold window. And still the fact always remained that Carina had lost her temper and had called Amy a Pharisee.

But suppertime came and passed. At last, it was bedtime, and Carina had Mommy alone.

"Mommy," the child at once began, "did you hear me call Amy a Pharisee—this afternoon when the clock was broken and we quarreled?"

"No, dear." Mommy hid a smile.

"Well, I did. And I was awfully angry. And—and I think I was really the Pharisee!"

"Oh no, you weren't, Carina. Don't fret. You were all three upset and not very nice to look at, with cross faces and snapping eyes. But after all, I don't think you couldn't be forgiven."

Mommy's laugh took much of Carina's trouble away. "Only, don't repeat the performance."

"I hope not to," said Carina. "I feel so mean, Mommy, when I think about it!"

"That's why you're not the Pharisee, darling. He was too pleased with himself for anything."

"'Two people went up to the temple area to pray; one was a Pharisee and the other was a tax collector.'[67] It's funny, Mommy, I never forget that part of the Bible," said Carina.

"They are verses that do stay with us somehow, Carina, like lines that rhyme. And the entire story is easily remembered and understood."

"I know the Pharisees were Jews who thought they were better than anybody else," said Carina. "But what else does it say, Mommy?"

"Our Lord rebuked them many times, sweetheart, besides in this parable of the Pharisee and the tax collector. He says they loved the first places at feasts and the first chairs in the synagogues and he calls them hypocrites and says they do not enter the Kingdom of Heaven. They were Jews who were very exact and particular about following the outward rules of their religion, but they did not serve God in their hearts. That is why Jesus calls them hypocrites. They pretended to be extra good, and made a great show of going to the temple and saying long prayers; but they were unjust and dishonest and took even from

---

[67] Luke 18:10

the support of poor widows. The mass of the people, seeing the many visits to the synagogue and the long prayers and severe faces of the Pharisees, considered them wonderful people, and honored them very much. You see, persons in this world may be deceived by appearances, and often are, but it is impossible to deceive God."

"And the tax collector, Mommy? What was he?"

"The tax collectors were terribly hated by the Jews, and in some cases, no doubt justly. They were supposed to be hard and cruel in their dealings when they collected the money for taxes, and were often suspected of forcing people to pay more than was the law. I think that no persons were more despised and detested, Carina, than these tax collectors. No one believed anything good about a tax collector; nobody trusted him. His business was considered a disgrace. In the parable, Jesus puts the respected, looked-up-to Pharisee and the hated tax collector together: 'Two people went up to the temple area to pray; one was a Pharisee and the other was a tax collector.' No sooner was the Pharisee in the temple, than he started in to show his state of mind. He had seen the tax collector entering the synagogue with him and the Pharisee's heart at once swelled with pride. Standing proudly, he prayed to God, beginning by saying, 'O God, I thank you that I am not like the rest of humanity.'[68] He went on to explain that the tax collector was like the rest of men, committing all sorts of sins against God's commandments. The Pharisee

---

[68] Luke 18:11

didn't mention anything about his own sins, Carina; he simply told all of the tax collector's."

"How mean!" exclaimed Carina.

"Very much worse than mean, dear, if you remember he was talking to almighty God. But let's say mean, and to tell somebody else's faults is as easy as it is mean. Having performed this easy confession of the tax collector's sins, the Pharisee slipped over to his own perfections. They were not really perfections, but he thought they were. They were merely some of the hypocrisy which marked the Pharisees. 'I fast twice a week,'[69] said the Pharisee, feeling that he was very good indeed, and that God must recognize his goodness; 'I pay tithes on my whole income,'[70] he finished, as though nothing more could possibly be expected of anybody. Tithes meant that the Pharisee gave the tenth of all he owned to the poor—as though Carina gave one penny out of every dime."

"I see, Mommy; I was going to ask you."

"I don't know whether the Pharisee stayed very long in the temple that day, but if he did, his prayer did not change. He told God of other people's sins and his own holiness, and he thanked God he wasn't like others.

"Now the tax collector was different. He felt that he was very unworthy to appear before God, he knew that he had done a great many things which were wrong, and had neglected to do most of the things which would please God. He was too humble to go

---

[69] Luke 18:12
[70] Luke 18:12

up to the front of the temple. Instead, he stood near the door at the back, and with his head bowed down he struck his breast and prayed, 'O God, be merciful to me a sinner.'[71] I'm sure that even the tax collector, if he had tried, could have remembered something good he had said or done in his life. But he didn't tell God anything about how good he was, or had been. Neither did he relate all the evil doings of his companions. The tax collector might have said there were thieves and murderers in the world, and lots of others worse than he, if he had had a proud heart like the Pharisee. But no, the tax collector was a sinner, and knew how often he had offended God. He did not begin to make any comparisons. What would be the use? God knew every heart. And it was sad but true that the tax collector himself was a sinner, whatever the rest of men might be. So his prayer went up to the throne of God, straight from a heart that was humble and sorry: 'O God, be merciful to me a sinner.'"

As Mommy paused for a moment, Carina's soft little arm went around Mommy's neck.

"I'm sorry about today," whispered Carina; "I don't want to be a Pharisee. If that Pharisee had thought of some very good people, much better than he was, 'stead of bringing up the poor tax collector, Mommy, he couldn't have felt so proud."

"That's a fine idea. If we compare at all, let's show ourselves how much worse we are than some others.

---

[71] Luke 18:13b

Then we'll be ready to pray with the tax collector—'O God, be merciful to me a sinner,' because, Carina, we all want the result our Lord said the tax collector's prayer obtained."

"Yes, Mommy?"

"Jesus said the tax collector went down to his house justified—which means forgiven—rather than the other. You see, the Pharisee's fasting and charity had not helped him after all, because his heart was filled with such pride that he thought that he could deceive not only the world, but God also about his hidden sins."

"Poor Pharisee!" said Carina. "Wasn't he silly?"

"Yes. He was a sort of coward, Carina, who could not be honest with himself. He was a pretender, a hypocrite, and God was not pleased with his prayer. When he left the temple, he had his reward: the people watched him with respect and admiration. But the despised tax collector went home with the peace of God in his heart, his faults forgiven, and the angels in heaven rejoicing because he, a sinner, had done penance."

"It is nice," said Carina, like one who very well understood, "to be forgiven. When you first get all worried, Mommy, and then you are all comfortable again, it really, truly is very nice."

"So we are fond of the tax collector as he seems very near ourselves. You are quite right, Carina—we know how he felt. Now close up those bright eyes and go to sleep—all forgiven and comfortable."

"Yes, Mommy dear. Good night!"

Discussion Questions

1. Have you ever said something you wished you could take back? Have you ever felt different about yourself after you said something mean or selfish? What can you do or say to make things better?

2. How are we sometimes "deceived by appearances"? Why is it important not to judge by what we see on the outside—without knowing a person's intentions?

3. Why is it important to compare ourselves only to Jesus rather than to others around us? How does this ensure more honesty in our own confession of our sins?

Growing In Holiness

Each day we must courageously look at our sins and failings. We must be honest and not make excuses for our thouhts, words, or actions. We must make firm amendments to change any habits that do not please Jesus. We must be quick to forgive others and to offer our forgiveness. As Christian Catholics, we have a high calling to be just like our Lord and Savior, Jesus Christ! Work each day to be more like him.

Searching Scripture – Luke 18:9-14

He then addressed this parable to those who were convinced of their own righteousness and despised everyone else. "Two people went up to the temple area to pray; one was a Pharisee and the other was a tax collector. The Pharisee took up his position and spoke this prayer to himself, 'O God, I thank you that I am not like the rest of humanity—greedy, dishonest, adulterous—or even like this tax collector. I fast twice a week, and I pay tithes on my whole income.' But the tax collector stood off at a distance and would not even raise his eyes to heaven but beat his breast and prayed, 'O God, be merciful to me a sinner.' I tell you, the latter went home justified, not the former; for everyone who exalts himself will be humbled, and the one who humbles himself will be exalted."

✓ Checking the Catechism

1. *What is the examination of conscience?* The examination of conscience is an earnest effort to recall to mind all the sins we have committed since our last worthy confession.

2. *How can we make a good examination of conscience?* We can make a good examination of conscience by calling to memory the commandments of God, the precepts of the Church, the seven capital sins, and the particular duties of our state in life, to find out the sins we have committed.

✦REVIEW✦ Adult Catechism

No. 422. [Justification] is the merciful and freely-given act of God which takes away our sins and makes us just and holy in our whole being. (See CCC Nos. 1987-1995 and 2017-2020.)

The Our Father

It was the night after Mommy told Carina about the Pharisee and the tax collector, and Carina was very still in Mommy's arms, having for a wonder, no question ready, no anxious little trouble for Mommy to settle.

"Tell me anything you like, tonight, Mommy," said Carina; "I like everything—if you tell it"—and her eyes looked up with the truest kind of flattery in them, at Mommy's smiling face.

"So very easy to please? What happened, Carina?"

"Nothing, Mommy." A queer, little twist pulled at Carina's lips and she suddenly turned her head, so the face was hidden against Mommy's arm—Carina was certainly very shy, whatever might be the reason.

"So Carina hides her little face and wriggles," her mother teased, "all about nothing."

"I," said Carina faintly, "was meek." It is very funny, but Carina is always much more upset at saying she was good, than at confessing she has been naughty.

"Lovely!" said Mommy. "What did you do?"

Carina's round face stole out of the hiding place in Mommy's arm.

"It was Grandma," said Carina. "She scolded me for losing her belt, and I really hadn't seen it for ever so long, Mommy. She lent it to me to play with, once, and when she couldn't find it she said I must have had it." Carina paused. She was getting near the hard part—the part where she had been meek.

"Well?" Mommy encouraged.

"I politely said I hadn't had it, although I was mad, awfully mad. I got red (I know because my face was all hot.), but I kept still, and soon Grandma said, 'I'm sorry I scolded, dear; the belt was in my closet.' And I was glad I knew about the *Blesseds*."

Mommy was glad, too. It is very unpleasant to be cross, and very unpleasant to see other people cross. If Carina always remembered that *Blessed* about meekness, her mother knew many little storms would be prevented.

'That's simply splendid," said Mommy, then, and she held Carina very closely for a little minute, while it was oh, so still! in the bedroom. The kind of stillness when the clock ticks soothingly, and you are exactly as happy as if you were singing at the top of your voice for joy. Suddenly, Daddy did begin to sing downstairs, and Carina stirred slightly.

"I love to know Daddy's there," said she dreamily.

"Yes," said Mommy. "But why, Carina?"

Mommy was curious to know whether the small daughter could really give any explanation of why she was glad when her father was home.

"Oh," said Carina comfortably, "Daddy's so big and strong and he loves us, and takes care of us—why, he's Daddy, don't you know? And Mommy and Carina are just girls."

Mommy's laugh floated all the way down to Daddy in the library.

"We'd be pretty lonely and helpless by ourselves, shouldn't we, dear? You've said exactly what I thought you would. And I wanted to hear you say it because that idea of the strength and protection of a father is the beginning of the Lord's Prayer. Let's talk about it tonight—the prayer Jesus said."

"Where did Jesus say it first, Mommy?"

"In that same Sermon on the Mount where we find the Eight Beatitudes. That sermon, Carina, if we thought over every one of its sentences, could keep us busy all our lives. When you have grown to be a big girl, you will read it again and again and always find more to think about. It is like a whole school of education. But it's a school where classes never end; they only keep on going higher and higher—the last class, Carina, graduates into heaven. There is a class for every year of our lives, if we stop to think about it, and in the end we go home to heaven to see the Master who has been teaching us all along from his Sermon on the Mount. You know how long boys and girls work and study to be ready to meet the world in society. Now all God's children upon earth, big and little, young and old—Carina, Daddy, Mommy, and everybody—are meant to be in that school

Jesus started when he talked to the people from the mountain. And if they study faithfully, and don't miss too many lessons, at the last they are prepared to meet Jesus in his kingdom of heaven. That's a wonderful way to graduate, isn't it, Carina?"

"Yes, Mommy," said Carina earnestly; "because fathers and mothers graduate, too, and little girls stay with them."

"Certainly. Heaven is the happiest sort of a family party. And the head of that great family of all the peoples of the world is God: As Jesus says, in the beginning of the Lord's Prayer 'Our Father.'"

"Who art in heaven," Carina said softly; "watching us, Mommy, and taking care of us, like Daddy, but up in heaven."

"And after calling him our Father, Jesus warns us about the respect and love we should have for that holy title. He at once adds, 'Hallowed be Thy name.' This loving, pitying Father is God who created us, and his name must in all ways be hallowed, which means reverenced, or treated as holy. God's name dare not be used lightly, nor in anger, nor in any way that does not honor our Father in heaven who holds the earth and sky in his hand and is adored by millions of angels. Think of his power, Carina, and of how little and weak we are. We couldn't draw one breath unless God permitted. We are entirely dependent upon his goodness and his strength. So with the adoring angels we say, 'Hallowed be Thy name.' It is the name of the Almighty One, the Holy One, who keeps us."

'The next part is "Thy kingdom come,"' said Carina a bit anxiously. "Mommy, does that mean I must want to die?"

"No, no, darling. 'Thy kingdom come' is how we ask God to take possession of our minds and hearts, and by guiding all of us under his rule, to make this world his kingdom, as well as heaven. You see, if we were all living under God's Will and never sinning against what he wishes us to do, the world would be always beautiful and peaceful, and like a part of heaven. Where God is king, no wrong can happen. Let's explain it this way, Carina: Wherever goodness is, the Kingdom of God in this world has come. And that it may come more and more, and always abundantly, we pray 'Your kingdom come.'"

"'Thy will be done on earth as it is in heaven,'" Carina went on. "That means we mustn't mind and be cross when we can't have things the way we want."

"It's the prayer we need most of all. Sometimes, it's awfully hard to say it with our whole hearts. We want something badly—we long for it like you longed for rich cake while you were sick, although my little girl knew very well it would be wrong and harmful for her to eat it. We need courage to pray 'Thy will be done on earth as it is in heaven.' In heaven, God's will is done by his angels and saints, who obey perfectly and with joy. You see that it means a whole lot to do God's will as they do. We are more likely to obey with some complaint, and a sort of grudge. So we are taught by our gentle Jesus that in obedience our models are the angels and saints. They never grow tired of doing the will of our Father in heaven, because his will is their delight."

"They never even think of being naughty," sighed Carina.

"No. And that we may be strong to do the will of our Father, here on earth where we often grow tired and discouraged, Jesus teaches us to pray 'Give us this day our daily bread.' That means not only our food, but everything necessary for the life of both soul and body. It takes in all our earthly or temporal needs, and every want of our souls as well. It means, give us, besides our food and clothes and homes, God's grace and his sacraments, to be strong, patient, and faithful. In a very special way, dear, 'our daily bread' means the Holy Communion, which Carina will receive some happy day when she is older.

"And forgive us our trespasses as we forgive those that trespass against us," Mommy continued. "There are some words, Carina, big people as well as little people are apt to let slip from the tongue without considering what very serious matters they are speaking about. Do you know what 'trespasses' means?"

'Yes, Mommy. I remember what you told me long ago: 'Trespasses' means our faults and sins—you said 'anything that is displeasing to God.' I think," said Carina regretfully, "that almost everybody has lots of trespasses."

"There's no doubt. And knowing how much patience we need from God, as we ask him to forgive us, we promise to pardon all our friends and relatives."

"And playmates," Carina broke in, "and their big

brothers who tease—and everyone.''

"Exactly. We tell our heavenly Father that we intend to forgive everybody who offends us, as we hope he will forgive our sins against him. And we want these forgiven completely, don't we? We don't want God to say 'I forgive you that fit of temper, but not this one.' So imagine how dreadful it is of us, poor unfortunate sinners, when we climb up high upon pride and declare, 'I won't forgive this person that mean act. I won't forgive another the hasty word.' If God took us exactly at our own words, he would say, 'You prayed to be forgiven the same way you pardoned others. You do not pardon them, and in my justice I will not forgive you.' That would be terrible, wouldn't it?"

"Yes indeed, Mommy. I'll try hard to forgive." Carina looked very earnest. She knew it was very often hard to excuse the faults of her small companions. But she knew, too, that Carina herself had many little tricks and traits not perfectly lovable. And she meant to begin to try with all her might to say—'Forgive us our trespasses as we forgive them that trespass against us,' as Jesus wished.

"The next petition, or request, is a cry to God for his assistance when we are in danger of disobeying him by sin. 'Lead us not into temptation, but deliver us from evil.' There will be evil in our way as long as the world lasts. Never forget, Carina, that this life is a test or a trial."

"Like an examination?" said Carina.

"That's a fine idea. It's an examination in which

we shall pass or fail. And if God did not help us by his grace, no one could do anything but fail. But while temptation will often be near us, God will bring us safely through. We hold his banner high as long as we keep out of sin, and nothing can bring it down into the dust except we willfully let it go. Temptation is never as strong as God. No matter how powerful it may appear, why, Carina, it has to run away at the sound of the holy name! Try to learn this: We are strong because of God. Temptation is weak because of God. He will never refuse to 'deliver us from evil.'"

'Then comes 'Amen,'" said Carina.

"'Amen' is Hebrew and means 'So be it.' All prayers end that way. The word is a sacred pledge that what was said is true and sincere. Sometimes Jesus began to speak by saying the solemn word 'Amen.' By doing so, he attracted the attention of the people in a special way. Now let us say 'Amen,' my darling, and may my little girl sleep well!"

Discussion Questions

1. Have you ever not defended yourself when someone accused you of something? Have you ever not accused someone else of doing something even when you were sure they had done it? Have you ever overlooked someone else's mistake without pointing it out to them? Share a time when you were meek.

2. What does it look like when you see others fighting? What do their faces look like? (Try to catch your face in a mirror the next time you are angry.) Can you feel the anger in the air? Is it necessary to respond to anger with your own anger? How else could you respond?
3. Talk about each phrase of the Our Father. Why is it important to pray this prayer each day? What are we asking for when we pray this prayer?

✠ Growing In Holiness

As we learn the virtue of meekness from Carina, we see how hard it is to share our successes in not defending ourselves. We see how hard it is to tell others all about our joys and successes. When we are meek, it is easier to share our sins and failings than it is to talk about the times we truly imitated Jesus. Work on developing the virtue of meekness by not saying that angry word, not defending yourself against an unfair accusation, by doing something nice for someone and not telling anyone about it.

📖 Searching Scripture – Matthew 6:9-15

"This is how you are to pray:

Our Father in heaven,
   hallowed be your name,
   your kingdom come,
   your will be done,
      on earth as in heaven.
Give us today our daily bread;

and forgive us our debts,
as we forgive our debtors;
and do not subject us to the final test,
but deliver us from the evil one.

If you forgive others their transgressions, your heavenly Father will forgive you. But if you do not forgive others, neither will your Father forgive your transgressions."

✓ Checking the Catechism

1. *Why is the Our Father the best of all prayers?* The Our Father is the best of all prayers because it is the Lord's Prayer, taught to us by Jesus Christ himself, and because it is a prayer of perfect and unselfish love.

2. *Why is the Our Father a prayer of perfect and unselfish love?* The Our Father is a prayer of perfect and unselfish love because in saying it we offer ourselves entirely to God and ask from him the best things, not only for ourselves but also for our neighbor.

★REVIEW★ Adult Catechism

No. 579. The *Our Father* is the "summary of the whole Gospel" (Tertullian), "the perfect prayer" (St. Thomas Aquinas). (See CCC Nos. 2761-2764 and 2774.)

Carina and the Presence of God

Carina, lying very still but with wide open eyes in her bed, was considering. Mommy sat beside her in the dark bedroom. And if Carina was the great asker of questions, Mommy was surely the best one in the world to answer—particularly in the quiet, dim bedroom where Carina had Mommy all to herself, just sitting there to be with her little girl and ready to talk about whatever was troubling or hurting or interesting Carina.

"Mommy," said Carina suddenly, "what is the 'Presence of God'?"

Her mother stirred slightly, a bit surprised that Carina had caught this expression.

"What do you think it means, little one?"

"I don't know, Mommy. Only it seems to me it's not the kind of presents you give me for Christmas. Is it, Mommy?"

"No, dear. 'The Presence of God' means the fact of God being with us, always and in all places. Don't you see, Carina, I am present with you now?"

Carina continued to consider. She was a truthful

child and not too proud to say she did not understand. Some little people are afraid of appearing stupid if they tell the truth and say they do not understand things. Those small girls and boys are to be pitied. Mommy would be very sad if Carina acted that way. So Mommy waited patiently while Carina thought the matter over.

"Yes," came Carina's answer at last; "it's easy to know you are here, Mommy dear. But God—" Carina paused in embarrassment.

"Well . . ." encouraged Mommy.

"You see," said Carina, with a grave air of apology, "God is so different from mothers!"

Mommy patted the puzzled, little head. "Now listen, Carina. You know I am with you as much of the time as I can manage?"

"Yes, Mommy."

"And you know that I wish I could spend more time with you. But sometimes I can't. I have to be at work when they expect me and sometimes meetings keep me away from you. I must keep the house in order, and shop for groceries and your little clothes. Every day there are many, many matters to keep me busy and away from you. So there are hours and hours when only my love and prayers can be with my little girl. At such times, I am not present."

Mommy paused till she heard a soft little "Yes, Mommy."

"For instance, at night—Mommy comes to look at you in your sleep, to kiss you and say a little prayer, and then Mommy has to fall asleep herself. The day's work is over, and Mommy, like Carina, is tired and would be sick if she could not sleep. During the time Mommy is fast asleep, she cannot watch you, nor care for you, nor help you."

Carina grasped Mommy's hand more tightly; she did not like the picture of Mommy being unable to take care of her.

"This is the way it is with Mommy. All her love and interest for you can't make it possible for her to be always with you, always guarding you and looking out for you. Only God can be present in every place and at all times. When Mommy is away, or busy in her room, or fast asleep, God is here with Carina. When the lights are out and the whole world is resting with closed eyes, God watches my little girl, exactly the same as in the light and bustle of the day. There is a beautiful line in one of the psalms, Carina."

"What are the psalms, Mommy, please?" Carina interrupted. "I know they are in the Bible, but what are they?"

"They are what we call the songs of the great King David. A psalm is a kind of prayer and hymn combined. David himself wrote most of them, and many of the rest were written for him. The Jews had a word in their language for psalms, meaning 'hymns of praise.' But I like to remember the prayer part, because they are both wonderful and beautiful prayers if we think about them. Well, Carina, in one of those splendid psalms there is a line like this: 'The Lord is the keeper of little ones.'[72] Doesn't that give you some idea of his Presence with you? He is keeping you, little one."

"No matter where I am," said Carina slowly, "or what I am doing."

"Exactly. It is strange, darling, that we ever forget this great but so simple fact. Whether we laugh or cry, or pray or play, or sleep or work, we are always in the Presence of God—always in the company of our heavenly Father, always under the eyes of our dear Jesus. Much more perfectly than Mommy with all her love can watch you, is God watching you, Carina. And to remember that we are in his sight—to try to understand what it means to pass our lives near him—is called attending to the Presence of God. Have I explained it to you, Carina?"

"I think so, Mommy. It means that God is always with me, and I must always be polite to him. It's not polite to forget visitors, Mommy. If I went visiting and people forgot me, I'd go home again."

"That's it, dear. But there's one of the great differences between what is possible for human beings to do, and something else that is impossible for them to do. Carina, you could leave any person on earth sooner or later. But you can never leave the Presence of God. As the Bible tells us, we can never flee from him. At the top of the highest mountain, or at the bottom of the sea, there is no spot where God is absent. Nothing is unknown to our heavenly Father—nothing is hidden from him—because he is present

---

[72] See Psalm 116:6 in the Douay-Rheims translation.

in all places. If the tiniest child in the world did something which it wished kept a secret, the child might be able to hide the secret from Daddy and Mommy and Grandma. But God would know. He knows our best thoughts and our kindest actions, our little pains and aches and disappointments, and he knows our worst faults, too."

"Oh dear!" sighed Carina.

"But he knows how hard it is sometimes to be good, darling, and he loves us tenderly and wants us to love him, and he never expects too much of us. When we have done what displeases him, when we have acted in a manner unfitting his Presence, if we are sorry and ask him to forgive us, he always will. He is the King of Kings and Creator of heaven and earth, but he is also our heavenly Father. He is never tired, and he never sleeps, and his care surrounds us every instant of our lives. You see, Carina, to realize the Presence of God is to begin to have something of heaven while we still live in this world. The angels see God always; so do the souls in heaven. They are forever praising God, face to face. We know he is present with us; they both know and see that Presence. So if we remember God is with us, we are taking part in the service the angels give him."

"And the angels will help us, won't they, Mommy, to be very polite to our heavenly Father?"

"Yes, dear. We'll ask our guardian angels to adore him with us—and for us, all the long night while we are asleep."

"Mommy, you say sometimes 'I wish I need never

have you out of my sight,' don't you?"

"I believe I do, dear. Why?"

"Because, you don't want me out of your sight, and God never does have me out of his sight."

"Quite right. And God's sight is the necessary one, the one that can keep my little girl from every danger. He sees not only you, but everything, that can do you good or harm. And knowing everything, he arranges our lives the best way for us to serve him. We can't control all the little things that make up our days. Why, even the weather sometimes changes our plans!"

"Yes," said Carina regretfully; "twice it rained and we couldn't have our picnic."

"Although we were all prepared," laughed Mommy. "That is what I mean. We make our plans, but God manages our lives. Sometimes he permits all our plans to succeed, other times he shows us, perhaps in even very little matters, that his will is not the same as ours."

"But he knows why," said Carina thoughtfully.

"Yes, he always knows why, and in heaven we too will know. Are you very sleepy, Carina?"

"Not so awfully," returned Carina, charmingly uncertain. "There was something else, Mommy. Tell me before I close my eyes tight. It was about 'delight' and 'children.'"

"I know what you mean. It's God's side of the 'Presence.' He says, 'My delight is to be with the children of men.'"[73]

_____

[73] See Proverbs 8:31 in the Douay-Rheims translation.

"Yes, that's it. God's glad to be here—with me." And the eyelids closed with a happy sigh.

Discussion Questions

1. What can we do to become more aware of God's Presence in our lives? How can an attitude of gratitude help?
2. How much of your day do you share with God? How many times do you talk to him throughout the day? Do you ask your angel to help you to praise God?
3. "We make our plans, but God manages our lives." How do you cooperate with God's plan for your life? When do you complain? Do you try to follow him and do his will? Is there any happiness in doing our own will without cooperating with God?

Growing In Holiness

Living in the Presence of God is "to begin to have something of heaven while we still live in this world" (page 161). It is another way of saying, "Thy kingdom come." Develop the habit of living in God's Presence and accepting his unconditional loving care for us by praying often: "My Jesus, I trust in you."

Searching Scripture – Matthew 28:20b, 2 Corinthians 6:16, and Matthew 18:10

". . . And behold, I am with you always, until the end of the age."

For we are the temple of the living God; as God said:
"I will live with them and move among them,
and I will be their God
and they shall be my people."

"See that you do not despise one of these little ones, for I say to you that their angels in heaven always look upon the face of my heavenly Father."

✓ Checking the Catechism

1. *If God is everywhere, why do we not see him?* We do not see God, because he is a pure spirit and cannot be seen with bodily eyes.
2. *Why can we not see God with the eyes of our body?* We cannot see God with the eyes of our body because they are created to see only material things, and God is not material but spiritual.
3. *Does God see us?* God sees us and watches over us.
4. *Is it necessary for God to watch over us?* It is necessary for God to watch over us, for without his constant care we could not exist.
5. *Does God know all things?* God knows all things, even our most secret thoughts, words, and actions.

★REVIEW★ Adult Catechism

No. 540. The Psalms are the summit of prayer in the Old Testament . . . [singing] of God's marvelous deeds in creation and in the history of salvation.

Why Carina Should Not Be Afraid

Carina was a very brave little girl in some ways: She would go upstairs all alone in the dark, she never screamed if she saw a dog, she did not hang her head and look silly when Mommy wished her to meet strangers. There were some ways she was even foolishly brave—but no, we will not say foolishly brave. Let us say there were times when Carina did not understand that what she did was dangerous, and so she went ahead with what might have cost her precious little life. Or, perhaps she might have been spared her life, but without her eyes, or an arm or a leg. Now Carina was a very strong, happy little girl and it would be terrible to suddenly find herself hurt so she could never be well and perfectly happy again.

One day, Mommy found Carina standing on a window sill. The sight was an awful one for Mommy. Carina was only six years old, and she did not understand that if she fell out into the street, she would either be killed or very dreadfully hurt. Mommy, praying very hard indeed, stole up behind the child and grabbed Carina firmly around her little waist.

"Oh!" cried Carina, greatly startled. When she looked up into Mommy's white, frightened face, Carina cried "Oh!" once more.

Carina was not brave when she climbed up and stood balancing on the window sill. She was only ignorant of danger. It is very sad to be ignorant, especially about how to take care of one's health. One thing Mommy has had to teach Carina is how to be afraid at the right time. Not to fear real danger is stupid and wrong.

But sometimes Carina was so timid that she made herself miserable; she would cling to Mommy and shut her eyes in perfect terror. It was too bad, and Mommy did not like to see her sensible, little girl work herself up into an unreasonable person. If a caterpillar happened to crawl over her, Carina would scream and tremble, as though a hungry lion had caught hold of her. No caterpillar in the world could eat Carina up. In fact, all the caterpillars in the world could not eat her. One little shove of Carina's chubby hand would send Mr. Caterpillar sprawling upon the ground. But it took Carina a long time to understand that a caterpillar is not the same thing as a hungry lion, and that a mere baby could send any caterpillar wriggling upon his back.

Then cows! Dear me, out in the country there was the gentlest cow that everyone could pet, but Carina would clasp Grandma's hand tightly and close her eyes if she only passed the field in which poor Mrs. Cow was standing under a tree. There was no sense in being afraid. Even a cross cow could not have jumped over the stone wall, and this was a cow that was gentle as a pet lamb. She mooed after Carina, because she was lonely in the pasture, and longed to be stroked and talked to. But Carina could not be coaxed to go near her.

However, nothing that frightened Carina could be compared with a thunderstorm. The child was miserable as long as one lasted. If it were supper time, Carina could eat nothing. If she had company, she sat down with folded hands, too polite to run away but too scared to try to play. If Mommy happened to be gone, the torture was complete. Grandma would only say "It's next to never that anyone gets killed," and Carina had heard the remark so often that the words had come to mean nothing to her.

Late one afternoon of a day when Mommy had gone to town, Carina was playing with three of her cousins at the brook. It had been hot, and the shade was very welcome down where the water went gurgling between the steppingstones.

The boys had built a dam with a waterfall, and now all four children were sailing bits of wood to the edge of the dam and watching them go over the falls and into the rough water below. Of course, they made plenty of noise, shouting every time one of their "boats" made the leap. Carina had not been any quieter than the others, but suddenly Grandma saw her stand perfectly still and listen with wide-open eyes and parted lips. Grandma at once knew what the matter was.

"It's thunder," said Carina. "I'm going home."

"Come on!" shouted the boys as big drops of rain

beat upon the trees above them. "Run, or you'll be soaked!"

Carina did not need to be told to run. She pulled Grandma with her, up the bank, across the lawn, up the porch steps, and into the house. In the hall, the child threw herself upon the couch and hid her face in the cushions. Carina had seen two bright flashes of lightning and did not want to see any more.

"And Mommy's away!" poor Carina told the pillows. "Oh, if only she would come home soon!"

"Sure," said Grandma, patting Carina's shoulder. "You needn't worry. It's next to never that anyone gets killed."

Then Grandma ran off to help shut the windows, and Carina lay shivering with fear, and longing terribly for Mommy, till half an hour later when the sun smiled through the last drops of the rain and a rainbow brightened the sky.

With the rainbow came Mommy and Daddy home from town.

"Oh!" sighed Carina, hugging Mommy. "I thought you'd never come! It was awful, Mommy, and I was so frightened!"

"Poor little Carina!" said Daddy. "Did you have any supper?"

"No, Daddy; I couldn't." She was hanging upon her father now.

"Then," said Daddy, "You shall have it with Mommy and me."

The solemn little face brightened at that, and they had a jolly time at table, the three of them.

But who would have expected another thunderstorm, just as Mommy was settling Carina and herself in the armchair for the bedtime story?

"Oh!" cried Carina, when the thunder began to rumble. "It's come back!" She caught her breath, every bit of fun gone out of her. "What shall I do?"

"Listen to a little story, Carina. Close your eyes if you like, but don't screw your face up into a knot. Try to listen to every word I say, will you, Carina?"

"Yes, Mommy," said Carina very faintly. She looked up into Mommy's face and just then a big crash of thunder came following upon some very lively lightning.

"It was pink," said Carina.

"Yes, and wonderfully beautiful. We never need be afraid, Carina, if we remember who makes the lightning and who controls it. The same God who made the earth and the sea, the God who created you and me and who loves us dearly, holds the lightning in his hand. There are some wonderful words in the Bible, dear, of how God 'Who has cupped in his hand the waters of the sea, and marked off the heavens with a span.'[74] That is to show us the power of God compared with our own weakness." Mommy paused as again the flashes of lightning played over the things in the room and the thunder roared back and forth, when the sound struck the hills.

"Don't tremble, darling. Think about God cupping in his hand the waters of the sea. Could you think that that almighty Father would forget us when he

---

[74] Isaiah 40:12a

sends the lightning? If you and I look at our weak little hands, we know they can do nearly nothing. But God's hand holds heaven and earth, and the lightning is as small to him as the light of a match would be to us.

"Not that our heavenly Father has a hand like ours. You might understand hand to mean 'power.' Those words in the Bible mean that all the great things in the world, all the forces and wonders, and the lightning and thunder, are no more in the wisdom and power of God, than we human beings consider things we can manage by a couple of fingers, or in the palm of one hand. That same verse in the Bible I was telling you about, goes on like this: 'Who has held in a measure the dust of the earth, weighed the mountains in scales and the hills in a balance?'[75] All these matters are immense to us, impossible to us. But they are God's work. His will keeps the earth in its place; he knows every stone in the mountains, every blade of grass upon the hills. And God sends the lightning, Carina, and directs its course. The little birds have gone to sleep, and the lightning will not touch them, because God cares for them. Is he less loving of my Carina?"

"No, Mommy. But, Mommy, sometimes people are killed by lightning."

"Very, very seldom, dear. We must have faith that God will not let us die that way. The Church prays that her children will not die by lightning or tempest."

"I didn't know that, Mommy." Carina's face was

---

[75] Isaiah 40:12b

losing its fear, although the storm was still very severe.

"We must be calm and full of faith. There was once a terrible storm at sea, a great tempest when Jesus was out in a boat with his disciples. The water was so wild that the waves washed completely over the boat, and the disciples, like my Carina, were dreadfully afraid. Jesus was with them, but he was weary after a hard day's labor for the multitudes, curing their diseases and teaching them, and he had fallen asleep. The disciples were not strong enough in faith to bear the storm calmly. They did not consider the weary Master, but went to him in terror and wakened him, crying 'Lord, save us! We are perishing!'"[76]

"'Lord, save us! We are perishing!'" Carina repeated as a crash made Mommy wait a second. But Carina watched the lightning now, and a little smile played around her lips. God managed the lightning, and God loved Carina.

"And listen to how Jesus answered them: 'Why are you terrified, O you of little faith?'[77] You see, it was only because they hadn't enough faith in the power and love of God that those disciples were terrified. Jesus was with them; they were safe—no matter how the ship rocked and the waters roared. But they were not willing to believe they were safe. And so Jesus rebuked them. He made them see their faith was a shaky sort, very fine in fair weather, but breaking down in a storm. Do we want Jesus to say the

---

[76] Matthew 8:25
[77] Matthew 8:26

same words to us, Carina, when a thunderstorm comes up—'Why are you terrified, O you of little faith'?"

"No, Mommy. I like to please Jesus," said the child.

"Then let's be full of trust in him. Let's see his power in the very storm itself, and know that the same power surrounds us. After rebuking the disciples for their weak faith, Jesus rose up in the boat and commanded the winds and the sea to be still. At once, there came a great calm. You see, God sends the calm at his will, as well as the tempest. The disciples were filled with wonder when the winds and waves ceased at the words of Jesus. The boat lay upon the quiet waters as though no storm had ever existed. The Master had commanded, the Lord who rules the wind and the sea, earth and heaven. And as calmness came upon the waters, peace and joy entered into the hearts of the disciples. Like the clouds had left the sky, doubt had left their minds. They saw clearly, Carina, that Jesus is almighty and with him his creatures are safe, in darkness as in light, in trouble as in joy, in the tempest as in the calm. Does he change, dear, because the lightning flashes?"

"No, Mommy," earnestly. "He is always Jesus."

"And we are always his children, to whom he says '. . . do not be afraid.'[78] Let's watch all his works with faith, Carina, and then we shall never fear. The storm is about over, and my little girl is very tired. You will fall asleep now?"

---

[78] Matthew 14:27b

"Yes, Mommy darling. I am not frightened any more—Jesus did not like the disciples to be frightened even when the waves went over the boat. Good night, Mommy."

👪 Discussion Questions

1. Why is it important to be afraid only at the right times? When is it important to be afraid? Name a time that fear showed a lack of faith in God's care.
2. Name some things that scare you. Why are you afraid of these things? What can you do to become less afraid? How does our fear hurt God?

✝ Growing In Holiness

Carina shows us that a sure knowledge of God's great love for us will decrease our fear of many things. Do not offend God by being afraid, but rather focus on his great love for you and his power to do all things. Remember, "Perfect love drives out fear." (1 John 4:18)

📖 Searching Scripture – Matthew 8:23-26

He got into a boat and his disciples followed him. Suddenly a violent storm came up on the sea, so that the boat was being swamped by waves; but he was asleep. They came and woke him, saying, "Lord, save us! We are perishing!" He said to them, "Why are you terrified, O you of little faith?" Then he got up, rebuked the winds and the sea, and there was great calm.

You may also wish to read Matthew 10:27-31 in which Jesus explains that we are not to be afraid.

✓ Checking the Catechism

1. *What is Faith?* Faith is a divine virtue by which we firmly believe the truths that God has revealed.
2. *Why do we believe God, hope in Him, and love Him?* We believe God and hope in Him because He is infinitely true and cannot deceive us. We love Him because He is infinitely good and beautiful and worthy of all love.

✱REVIEW✱ Adult Catechism

No. 380. Prudence disposes reason to discern in every circumstance our true good and to choose the right means for achieving it. (See CCC No. 1806 and 1835.)

St. Joseph

Mommy and Aunt Grace had been talking of patron saints, and Carina had heard what was said. You see, one of the cousins had had a new little baby and there was quite a good deal of excitement about choosing a name for it. Aunt Grace was to be godmother, and she hoped they would not give the little one what she called a "silly" name.

"One grandfather's named John, and the other Joseph," Mommy remarked. "Could that child find better patrons than St. John and St. Joseph? And the grandfathers would be delighted."

"Certainly," laughed Aunt Grace—who had not been married very long, and who seemed more like a little girl to Carina than a really-truly-grown-up lady. "Isn't my own second name Josephine, and hasn't St. Joseph been good to me? I even got along without grandfathers and grandmothers."

At that, Carina gave Aunt Grace a sudden hug. If St. Joseph had anything to do with Aunt Grace being so pretty and sweet and jolly, Carina agreed that he had been very good to her indeed.

But it would be simply terrible not to have any grandfathers and grandmothers.

"I haven't his name," Mommy said, "but he has always been my patron, nevertheless."

"Why?" Carina was about to ask. Only the telephone rang, and the little conversation was interrupted because Mommy had to talk with her friend.

But of course, Carina was ready with her question at bedtime.

"Mommy, why is St. Joseph your patron?"

"You little mischief, you never forget a question, do you?"

"Sometimes. But not questions about stories."

"Oh, I see. Well, I have St. Joseph for my patron because he had all the gifts I'd like to get a little scrap of. Besides, he had the earthly care of the Holy Family for his duty—and, Carina, he had the happiest kind of a death."

"Seems to me," said Carina dolefully, "no death could be happy."

"My little girl thinks that because she doesn't understand. Death for us, Carina, must mean going to live with God, our Father in heaven. It's going home, never to be lonely any more, nor cold, nor tired, nor discouraged, nor in pain. And how did St. Joseph die?"

"I don't know, Mommy." Carina was trying to think of a nice way.

"He died in the arms of Jesus and Mary. The Blessed Mother was to live many years longer than her divine Son, but St. Joseph left the little family before Jesus died. When St. Joseph went home to heaven, he was the first to break the circle at Nazareth, and he was taken before the heavy sorrows came to Jesus and Mary. No death was ever so beautiful or so joyous. St. Joseph went from the arms of the Savior straight to God the Father. To no one before or since was such a favor granted. And it is because of that beautiful death of St. Joseph that the Church made him the Patron of a Happy Death. We put our last hour upon earth into St. Joseph's keeping, darling, certain that he will not fail us when we need him.

"But we began at the end, Carina. There are a great many more favors for which we look to dear St. Joseph, besides a happy death. He was the foster-father of Jesus. He was the husband of Mary, and as husband and father he bore the burdens of the household. St. Joseph worked hard at the humble trade of a village carpenter, to supply food and clothing for his dear ones. It was a wonderful privilege to work for Jesus and Mary—to provide for the Creator, who made everything and to whom earth and sky belonged, and for his holy mother. People think it a sort of honor to be employed in the service of our president or in fact, Carina, anybody even a wee bit more famous or powerful or rich than most persons."

"And Jesus made all those people out of dust," said Carina, "and they live only as long as Jesus lets them?"

"Exactly. Yet they are honored and loved and served with a kind of happy pride. People boast of a position in the household of a king. Some will brag because their master is a millionaire. Now there is truly one reason—no, there are two reasons—why every human being is worthy to be loved and honored. Can you guess them?"

"No, Mommy."

"You know what the catechism says, that God made us to be happy with him forever in heaven. That is the first reason, and the second is that Jesus died to obtain heaven for us. It wouldn't do to refuse to honor a creature who was on the way to live with God, and for whom Jesus hung upon the Cross, would it?"

"No indeed," Carina heartily agreed. "I don't want any little girl to be horrid to my company—and we're all God's company some day in heaven, if we're good, aren't we, Mommy?"

"Yes—and that some day won't ever end. Well, St. Joseph was serving the King of Kings and Lord of Lords. He was laboring for the Son of God himself, and for the Immaculate Mother."

"What does 'maculate mean?" Carina suddenly asked.

"It means without a spot. God kept his mother from every stain of sin. She did not need Baptism like other children. You see, Carina, the great miracle was that Jesus was her Child, and connected with that, was a miracle not nearly so big, that Mary was not touched by sin."

"Because," said Carina, who was a sensible little thing, "God's mother couldn't be. It wouldn't have been right to Baby Jesus."

Mommy kissed the serious little face. "Quite right. And to go back to St. Joseph, it wasn't any easy, grand way he supported the Holy Family. He did hard, poorly-paid work. He may have been anxious very often, dear, about that little income necessary to provide for his household. It is because he had worldly care and responsibility that he is the Patron of Temporal Needs. Don't look troubled at the hard word: 'temporal' means relating to time, and our temporal needs, Carina, are food, clothes, money—anything it is well for us to have while we are living here on earth. In this world, you know, we live in time; in heaven we shall live in eternity. So when time ends, temporal needs will pass away. Does my little girl understand?"

"Yes, Mommy; temporal needs are the things we need here."

"Health, employment, success in what we try to do—all these things we can pray for through St. Joseph. Then, he is also the Patron of the Universal Church. Being the foster-father of Jesus, we feel sure he will act a father's part with all who follow Jesus. And, Carina, think how wise St. Joseph must be! He lived with God. He saw the Eternal Wisdom every hour in the day. You know how we copy those we love and respect—you copy me a whole lot, Carina —and you can imagine, at least a little bit, how St. Joseph studied Jesus. So we pray to a wise, as well as a loving, father when we pray to St. Joseph. I love to picture him working and thinking always, about that divine Child who was the Light of the home and at the same time the Light of the world. All children are so precious, Carina, and Jesus had everything that attracts us in them, besides the perfection of God himself. Don't you feel that St. Joseph must have talked very little, he was so busy watching Jesus?"

"I think so, Mommy. But," a bit bashfully, for Carina rarely disagreed with Mommy, "if I saw Jesus, I'd tell him everything. And I'd ask him lots."

"I'm sure you would. And he would answer you lovingly, as he always did the little children. Now, close your eyes and see him at Nazareth, near the Blessed Mother and St. Joseph, and tell him all you would tell him if you had lived with the Holy Family."

Carina dropped her eyelids with a smile. Presently, she looked up eagerly.

"I made the picture, Mommy. Is St. Joseph very old?" doubtfully.

"Rather old, and very gentle. Stately, too, I think, like one who associates constantly with the King. Above all, he is fatherly, and as a tender father watches over us, his children. Do you wonder I want him for my patron, Carina?"

"No, Mommy; I'm going to take him, too." Carina closed her eyes and clasped her chubby hands. "Dear St. Joseph," she prayed, "take good care of Carina, for Baby Jesus' sake. Amen."

Discussion Questions

1. Did you know that death means going home? Life on earth is temporary; our real home is heaven. What importance do you put on earthly things?

Are they more important than those of heaven?
Do you spend enough time preparing for your life
after death?
2. What are your temporal needs? What are your
spiritual needs? Both are important. Do you give
them both adequate time and thought?

✝ Growing In Holiness

A patron saint can be any saint whose name we
share (either through our given name or the name
we choose at Confirmation), upon whose feast day
we are born, who is the patron of our occupation, or
whom we have "adopted" because we admire and
want to imitate him or her. Who is your patron saint?
Learn more about this saint and try to imitate his or
her holy habits more faithfully. Compose a short
prayer to your patron saint. Pray to him/her often
asking for his/her help in your daily trials, joys, and
temptations.

✓ Checking the Catechism

1. *Who was the foster father or guardian of our Lord
while on earth?* St. Joseph, the husband of the
Blessed Virgin, was the foster-father or guardian
of our Lord while on earth.
2. *Why must we take more care of our soul than of
our body?* We must take more care of our soul
than of our body, because in losing our soul we
lose God and everlasting happiness.
3. *What must we do to save our souls?* To save our
souls, we must worship God by faith, hope, and

charity; that is, we must believe in him, hope in him, and love him with all our heart.

REVIEW **Adult Catechism**

No. 205. After death, which is the separation of the body and the soul, the body becomes corrupt while the soul, which is immortal, goes to meet the judgment of God . . . (See CCC Nos. 992-1004 and 1016-1018.)

The Feast of All Saints

Carina had had a party—a most beautiful party with flowers and lights on the table, and very good things to eat, and a clever man afterwards who sang and told stories and made the children laugh so hard!

There were a great many children. Carina would have said, her eyes very big, "Hundreds and hundreds, seems to me." But things often seemed more to the little girl than they were in fact. Mommy knew, because Mommy wrote the invitations, and Mommy said, "We asked fifty, and all are here except three." And, indeed, forty-seven children are a great many for a six-year-old to consider. Why, Carina could not remember half the names! Several of the nice little girls and boys who greeted her, she was quite positive she had never before seen. Here, Mommy again came to the rescue. There were cousins from Brooklyn, more cousins from Orange, some very pretty little girls who, Mommy said, were her "dearest girlfriend's children," some tall boys who teased and would not play with any but the very biggest girls. Oh, there were too many for the flushed, happy, confused Carina to recognize or remember!

But it was lovely, and everyone was delighted.

Now the guests had all gone, and Carina and her mother were alone.

"No story tonight for my little daughter?" asked Mommy.

"Oh, yes, indeed," protested Carina; "only perhaps not a very long one," she acknowledged.

"Well, do you know what the party made me think of, dear?"

"No, Mommy," and Carina settled herself expectantly.

"There were so many children, and they were so different in appearance and manners and disposition, but all so joyous, that I had to think of heaven, Carina. You know we celebrated the Feast of All Saints last week, and that feast, in my mind, is like a party in heaven. Perhaps no two saints are exactly alike. There are the great saints, the Apostles and martyrs and all those the Church has recognized; there are the angels and archangels, in the court of the Queen of Saints, Mary, the mother of Jesus. We cannot imagine the glory and beauty of even that assemblage of special names we know and love. But now think, Carina, of all the others!"

"How many, Mommy?" curiously. Forty-seven had seemed so very many!

"We don't know exactly, Carina. But we know there are thousands and thousands. The Bible tells us, '. . . a great multitude, which no one could count, from every nation, race, people, and tongue.'[79] From this, we may be sure that of every people that ever lived some are with God, praising him forever; clothed with white robes, and palms in their hands. Our own relations must be there, Carina, standing 'before the throne and before the Lamb.'"[80]

"Who is Jesus!" interjected Carina. "'. . . the Lamb of God, who takes away the sins of the world?'"[81]

"Yes, daughter. And why are all those saints, those we know and those whom no one on earth even remembers, so happy, darling?"

"Because they are with God, Mommy, and, because," slowly, "they never can be naughty or sorry anymore."

"That is quite right, little one. Sin and pain are gone when we reach heaven and join that glorious crowd of saints. There is no more hunger, nor thirst, nor weariness. God shall wipe away all tears from our eyes. And above everything, Carina, we shall see our Father face to face. We shall understand the things which we can't understand now, and we shall rejoice forever in the peace of God."

"It won't be only like going to sleep, Mommy, will it? 'Cause when I'm asleep—well, I'm good, Mommy, but I'm not really 'joying myself like at the party. I only forget everything."

"No, dear, heaven is not a place of sleep, although sometimes people—big folks like Mommy—get so

---

[79] Revelation 7:9
[80] Revelation 7:9
[81] John 1:29

tired of the troubles of this life that they are apt to think of heaven simply as a place of rest."

"I don't like to rest," objected Carina, very weary indeed, but inclined to begrudge the time she was obliged to spend "forgetting everything."

"Resting is not having a happy day, Mommy, like this was."

"No," thoughtfully. "Your little brain has caught a big idea, Carina. To be truly happy we must know what we are doing—not be unconscious of everything."

"Like I was in the scarlet fever," suggested Carina.

"Yes," amused, "to be like that is not enjoying ourselves, surely. Now, dear, think of the happiest day you ever had."

"Today," promptly.

"Well, think of today. And add all the pleasure of this day to all the pleasures everyone has experienced since God made Adam and Eve. Now, if you could imagine all that joy, it could not be even near enough to be compared with the happiness of heaven. Besides, dear, delights we have in this world pass away. Think how you waited for the party, how Mommy prepared, and now the day is over. We've only the memory of the party, Carina."

"But I can think about it a very long time," said Carina cheerfully.

"Yes, that is one of our consolations. In heaven, though, our happiness will exist forever. There won't be any dread left of disappointment or mistake or delay. We'll be safe, Carina—safe in the arms of Jesus!

We'll be celebrating a Feast of All Saints, our party in heaven, without change or interruption. And, little one, not only we ourselves shall be happy; everyone we have known and loved will be happy with us. Sometimes we see people sad, or in pain, or disturbed about something, and our own hearts sink out of sympathy for them. In heaven, we shall see all our dear ones joyous and beautiful, their worries and ills gone like their faults have gone, in the perfection of the life with God."

Mommy paused; her thoughts had carried her away from the facts of the dusky bedroom and she suddenly discovered that the little daughter was already fast asleep and perhaps dreaming of the Holy City with the gates of pearl.

Discussion Questions

1. Carina's mother tells her, "Perhaps no two saints are exactly alike." Name several saints that you know. How are they different? How are they alike? Who is your favorite saint? Why?

2. In heaven, "We shall understand the things which we can't understand now, and we shall rejoice forever in the peace of God." What are some things you don't understand now that you look forward to understanding in heaven? What would it be like to "rejoice forever in the peace of God"?

3. Describe what the Holy City with gates of pearl looks like to you. What will it feel like to be there?

✝ Growing In Holiness

"To be truly happy we must know what we are doing—not be unconscious of everything." Many times we do things out of habit—without really thinking about what we are doing or saying. Try to consciously be aware of doing and saying all you do and say for the glory of God. Try to stay away from "automatic pilot"— and bad habits. Draw closer to God by living in his loving presence at all times. Then, you are well on the road to joining the saints in heaven!

📖 Searching Scripture – Revelation 7:9-17

After this I had a vision of a great multitude, which no one could count, from every nation, race, people, and tongue. They stood before the throne and before the Lamb, wearing white robes and holding palm branches in their hands. They cried out in a loud voice:

> "Salvation comes from our God, who is seated on
>   the throne,
> and from the Lamb."

All the angels stood around the throne and around the elders and the four living creatures. They prostrated themselves before the throne, worshiped God, and exclaimed:

> "Amen. Blessing and glory, wisdom and thanks
>   giving,
> honor, power, and might
> be to our God forever and ever. Amen."

Then one of the elders spoke up and said to me, "Who are these wearing white robes, and where did they come from?" I said to him, "My lord, you are the one who knows." He said to me, "These are the ones who have survived the time of great distress; they have washed their robes and made them white in the blood of the Lamb.

For this reason they stand before God's throne
    and worship him day and night in his temple.
The one who sits on the throne will shelter them.
They will not hunger or thirst anymore,
    nor will the sun or any heat strike them.
For the Lamb who is in the center of the throne
    will shepherd them
and lead them to springs of life-giving water,
and God will wipe away every tear from their
    eyes."

✓ Checking the Catechism

1. *What is heaven?* Heaven is the state of everlasting life in which we see God face to face, are made like him in glory, and enjoy eternal happiness.
2. *In what does the happiness in heaven consist?* The happiness in heaven consists in seeing the beauty of God, in knowing him as he is, and in having every desire fully satisfied.
3. *What is the communion of saints?* The communion of saints is the union which exists between the members of the Church on earth with one another, and with the blessed in heaven and with the suffering souls in Purgatory.

✱REVIEW✱ Adult Catechism

No. 209. By "heaven" is meant the state of supreme and definitive happiness. Those who die in the grace of God . . . see God "face to face." (See CCC Nos. 1023-1026.)

More RACE for Heaven Products

RACE for Heaven study guides use the saint biographies of Mary Fabyan Windeatt to teach the Catholic faith to all members of your family. Written with your family's various learning levels in mind, these flexible study guides succeed as stand-alone unit studies or supplements to your regular curriculum. Thirty to sixty minutes per day will allow your family to experience:

- ☑ The spirituality and holy habits of the saints
- ☑ Lively family discussions on important faith topics
- ☑ Increased critical thinking and reading comprehension skills
- ☑ Quality read-aloud time with Catholic "living books"
- ☑ Enhanced knowledge of Catholic doctrine and the Bible
- ☑ History and geography incorporated into saintly literature
- ☑ Writing projects based on secular and Catholic historical events and characters

Purchase these guides individually or in the following grade-level packages. (Grades are determined solely on the length of each book in the series.)

Grades 3-4: *St. Thomas Aquinas, The Story of the "Dumb Ox"; St. Catherine of Siena, The Girl Who Saw Saints in the Sky; Patron Saint of First Communicants, The Story of Blessed Imelda Lambertini;* and *The Miraculous Medal, The Story of Our Lady's Appearances to St. Catherine Labouré*

Grade 5: *St. Rose, First Canonized Saint of the Americas; St. Martin de Porres, The Story of the Little Doctor of Lima, Peru; King David and His Songs, A Story of the Psalms;* and *Blessed Marie of New France, The Story of the First Missionary Sisters in Canada*

Grade 6: *St. Dominic, Preacher of the Rosary and Founder of the Dominicans; St. Benedict, The Story of the Father of the Western Monks; The Children of Fatima and Our Lady's Message to the World;* and *St. John Masias, Marvelous Dominican Gate-keeper of Lima, Peru*

Grade 7: *The Little Flower, The Story of St. Therese of the Child Jesus; St. Hyacinth, The Story of the Apostle of the North; The Curé of Ars, The Story of St. John Vianney, Patron Saint of Parish Priests;* and *St. Louis de Montfort, The Story of Our Lady's Slave*

Grade 8: *Pauline Jaricot, Foundress of the Living Rosary and the Society for the Propagation of Faith; St. Francis Solano, Wonder-Worker of the New World and Apostle of Argentina and Peru; St. Paul the Apostle, The Story of the Apostle to the Gentiles;* and *St. Margaret Mary, Apostle of the Sacred Heart*

The Windeatt Dictionary: Pre-Vatican II Terms and Catholic Words from Mary Fabyan Windeatt's Saint Biographies explains over 450 Catholic terms and expressions used in this popular saint biography series. Indispensable in expanding knowledge and practice of the Catholic faith, this book provides a ready access for the Catholic vocabulary words used in the RACE for Heaven Windeatt study guides. This dictionary also includes a Catholic book report resource that contains suggestions for forty-five Catholic book reports: fourteen writing projects, ten book report activities, and twenty-one topics for saint biographies.

Graced Encounters with Mary Fabyan Windeatt's Saints: 344 Ways to Imitate the Holy Habits of the Saints is a compilation of the "Growing in Holiness" sections of RACE for Heaven's Catholic study guides for the Windeatt saint biography series and presents 344 examples of saintly behavior, one for nearly every chapter in each of these twenty biographies. Enhance your encounter with the saints by practicing the models of devotion, service, penance, prayer, and virtue offered in this guide.

Communion with the Saints: A Family Preparation Program for First Communion and Beyond in the Spirit of St. Therese imitates St. Therese of the Child Jesus and her family who studied and prayed for sixty-nine days in anticipation of Therese's First Holy Communion. Modeling this preparation, the *Communion with the Saints* program will help any family find renewed fervor in the reception of the Eucharist. This resource includes a chapter-by-chapter study of the following four books:

- *The Little Flower, The Story of Saint Therese of the Child Jesus*—to provide the foundation of God's love for us and to encourage a desire for holiness

- *The Children of Fatima and Our Lady's Message to the World*—to show the sinfulness of our world and the need to avoid sin

- *The Patron Saint of First Communicants, The Story of Blessed Imelda Lambertini*—to inspire devotion to the Sacrament of Holy Communion

- *The King of the Golden City* by Mother Mary Loyola —to illustrate Jesus' Presence as a source of grace necessary to live a holy life

Each of the sixty-nine days of preparation includes read-aloud selections with enrichment activities, meditational readings, catechism lessons, and plenty of practical application to promote a growth in holiness and sanctity. Weekend suggestions include a list of over thirty-five family projects. The use of *My First Communion Journal* is encouraged with this program.

My First Communion Journal in Imitation of Saint Therese of the Child Jesus provides a lasting keepsake of a child's First Holy Communion. Saint Therese of the Child Jesus and her family studied and prayed for sixty-nine days prior to Therese's First Holy Communion. This journal imitates that family model of preparation for the reception of the Most Holy Eucharist. Each daily entry contains a stanza of a poem composed by Saint Therese, a quotation from Saint Faustina Kowalska's diary (*Divine Mercy in My Soul*), or a Scripture quotation. Two weekly themes—a floral theme in imitation of Saint Therese and a battle theme molded from the teachings of Saint Paul—are offered with accompanying weekly passages from Scripture suitable for memorization. This journal may be completed in conjunction with the *Communion with the Saints* program or used separately.

The King of the Golden City Study Edition is a new edition of a book that was originally published in 1921. This treasure of a book was written in response to a student's appeal for instructions along with "little stories" to help her prepare for Holy Communion. To fulfill this request, Mother Loyola of the Bar Convent in York, England, wrote a simple story that illustrates Jesus' desire to share an intimate relationship with each one of His children. This new edition contains some updated language but, quite deliberately, does not contain any pictures. Readers, as they progress through this story, will form a mental image of their King, one as unique and personal as their own relationship with Him. The study sections assist with the allegory, connect to the Bible as well as to the catechism, and explore the art of prayer in the spirit of the three Carmelite Doctors of the Church. Although written over eighty-five years ago for a young child, this book remains a timeless masterpiece of Catholic literature suitable for all ages. (Also available as a study guide only)

The Good Shepherd and His Little Lambs Study Edition is a simply told Catholic tale of four children who meet with their beloved aunt for "First Communion talks." More than a story, it is a First Communion primer that takes the tenets of the catechism and, through naturally-flowing conversations, relates them in the language of little ones to authentic Christian living. As Mrs. Bosch explains, "We might learn the catechism all the way through beautifully, and at the end find ourselves still very stiff and clumsy about loving our Lord. When He comes to us, we don't want to welcome Him into our souls only with answers out of the catechism, do we?" Enriched by appropriate Biblical passages, points of doctrine, and prayers, this story-primer is an enjoyable and effective read-aloud that will prepare the Good Shepherd's little lambs to worthily receive Him in the Holy Eucharist.

A Reconciliation Reader-Retreat: Read-Aloud Lessons, Stories, and Poems for Young Catholics Preparing for Confession provides a basic doctrinal explanation and review of the Sacrament of Reconciliation as well as a Gospel examination of conscience—a seven-day read-aloud formation retreat. To help the lessons come alive and to enable young Catholics to more readily apply these doctrines to their own daily lives, the lessons have been supplemented with pertinent short stories and poems. Each lesson contains reflection questions, a family prayer, and a "Gospel Examination of Conscience" that is formulated according to the dictates of the *Catechism of the Catholic Church*. This reader-retreat will not only enrich and deepen the sacramental experience for each member of your family but it will also provide several tools to help you recommit to leading a virtuous life and to grow together in holiness.

Alternative Book Reports for Catholic Students contains forty-five book report ideas to encourage critical thinking for ages seven to fourteen. These ideas are intended to provoke a reflection on those themes and topics that support and encourage Catholic living as well as some that may conflict with our Faith. Many report topics require an examination of our personal faith life and prompt us to take lessons from the saints to strengthen our own faith in God. The suggested activities vary from written exercises to creative art projects and include twenty-one topics specifically designed for saint biographies. Other activities can be used within a group or family.

Reading the Saints: Lists of Catholic Books for Children Plus Book Collecting Tips for the Home and School Library (formerly entitled *Saintly Resources*) is a valuable tool for Catholic home educators, classroom teachers, and collectors of Catholic juvenile books. *Reading the Saints* will help you discover living books from such popular out-of-print Catholic juvenile series as Catholic Treasury, Vision Books, and American Background Books as well as current series books for young Catholics. Use this book to find:

- Over 800 Catholic books listed by author, series, reading level, century, and geographical location

- More than 275 authors of saint biographies, historical fiction, and poetry written for Catholic juvenile readers

- Publishers of Catholic children's books, present and past

- Helpful advice for collecting and caring for used books

- Hundreds of age-appropriate, accessible living books to enrich your study of the Catholic Church's rich heritage of saints and notable Catholic historical figures

- Information on how to build and maintain your own library of Catholic juvenile books

- Inspiring quotations about book collecting, reading, and the love of books

The Outlaws of Ravenhurst Study Edition contains a classic story of the persecution of Scottish Catholics that was first written in 1923 and was revised and reprinted in 1950. This 2009 edition of Sr. M. Imelda Wallace's *Outlaws of Ravenhurst* contains the revised story of 1950 plus chapter-by-chapter aids to assist readers in assimilating the book's strong Catholic elements into their wn lives. The study section focuses on critical thinking, integration of biblical teachings, and the study of the virtuous life to which Christ calls us as mature Catholics. With its emphasis on virtues (theological and moral plus the gifts and fruits of the Holy Spirit), the spiritual and corporal works of mercy, and the Beatitudes, *Outlaws of Ravenhurst Study Edition* is a fun and effective catechetical tool for Catholics preparing for the Sacrament of Confirmation. (Also available as a study guide only)

The Family that Overtook Christ Study Edition: The Story of the Family of St. Bernard of Clairvaux is an excellent read for young adults who are preparing to receive the Sacrament of Confirmation. In this exciting chronicle of the life of twelfth-century knights, we have an entire family of nine saints who lay before us their individual means of achieving intimate union with Christ. Learn with the Fontaines family how to supernaturalize the natural, develop a God-consciousness, and attain sanctity by being yourself. Perfect for high-school read-aloud (or adult study), this new study edition has over 250 footnotes for increased comprehension and provides discussion/meditation points to promote the art of spiritual conversation. The appendix lists formulas of Catholic doctrine that are essential for confirmands not only to know but also to incorporate into their own spiritual lives.

A Confirmation Reader-Retreat: Read-Aloud Lessons, Stories and Poems for Young Catholics utilizes chapters from two excellent out-of-print Catholic books for children (*I Belong to God, Great Truths in Simple Stories for Children and Lovers of Children* by Lillian Clark; and *Children's Retreats in Preparation for First Confession, First Holy Communion, and Confirmation* by Rev. P.A. Halpin). This book provides a basic doctrinal review of the Sacrament of Confirmation as well as prayer experiences— a nine-day read-aloud retreat/novena. The reprinted material has been supplemented with short stories and poems that provide insights in applying catechetical doctrines to the daily life of young Catholics. Each lesson concludes with "I Talk with God"—a section that encourages readers (of all ages) to deepen their relationship with each of the Three Persons of the Blessed Trinity. Reflection questions promote the habit of spiritual conversation within your family—to encourage family members to discuss holy topics— and to help you grow together in holiness. Additionally, a traditional novena to the Holy Spirit is included.

To Order: Email info@RACEforHeaven.com or place an order from RACEforHeaven.com. Discover, MasterCard, VISA, PayPal, American Express, checks, and money orders are accepted.

www.ingramcontent.com/pod-product-compliance
Lightning Source LLC
Chambersburg PA
CBHW031254090426
42742CB00007B/453